W9-BPJ-917

Successfully Unemployed

The 16 Real-Life Lessons You **MUST** Learn Before You Quit Your Job and Live the Life of Your Dreams

By **Dustin Heiner**

Copyright

Master Passive Income
www.masterpassiveincome.com

Published by Triune Publications
Printed in the United States of America

ISBN-10: 0-9975155-8-9
ISBN-13: 978-0-9975155-8-9

DEDICATION

This book is dedicated to all of you who are on the path to quitting your job.

Never give up. Never stop growing. Never stop living.

It will all be worth it in the end.

Contents

READ THIS FIRST

A FREE BONUS FOR YOU!

JUST TO SAY THANK YOU FOR BUYING THIS BOOK, I'D LIKE TO GIVE YOU TWO BONUSES ABSOLUTELY **FREE**

- BONUS 17TH LESSON: MANAGING YOUR BUSINESS FINANCES

- THE SUCCESSFULLY UNEMPLOYED WORKBOOK

DOWNLOAD THESE AMAZING BONUSES FOR
"Successfully Unemployed"
100% FREE!

DOWNLOAD FREE INSTANTLY HERE
http://www.masterpassiveincome.com/SUBonus

CHAPTER ONE
FIRST AND FOREMOST

"The older I get the more wisdom I find in the ancient rule of taking first things first. A process which often reduces the most complex human problem to a manageable proportion."

- Dwight D. Eisenhower

Wantrepreneurs dream about quitting their job. Entrepreneurs actually do it.

From elementary school on, we are all taught that we need to get a good job to provide for our family and retire when we are 68 years old with a good pension, 401k, or some other retirement plan. The HUGE problem with that is you have already passed up your prime years working for someone else, making them rich. Why not retire at age 35 and live the rest of your life free from your job? It is possible and there is a way to be successfully unemployed.

The day I quit my job was one of the best days of my life. I was terrified, but I had planned 9 years for that day. When I was 27 years old, I made a commitment to myself to quit in 10 years. From that day forward, I was dedicated to the end goal of quitting my job. Going through this process, I learned a lot. What to do and what NOT to do.

When you quit your job, will you do it well? Will you set yourself up to be successful or will you be forced to get a job again? Fortunately, you found the book that will help you become successfully unemployed and never work for someone again. By learning these lessons that I had to figure out the hard way, you will be able to quit even sooner than you think. If I would have learnt these lessons, I would have quit 2 years earlier than I did.

Successfully Unemployed is your guide to help you understand what to do before you quit your job and go it alone, relying only on your business income to live on. These lessons have been proven to help many people quit their jobs successfully, be unemployed, and live their dream life. Those who have already started their business and are close to taking the leap of faith (in themselves) will benefit from following the path I have laid out in this book. The path to quitting your job has already been expertly navigated and will help you learn how to escape your job successfully.

As a lifetime student of business, passive income, and master of the art of using passive income to make money, I've already quit my job. Now, I provide for my family solely on passive income from many businesses I built and continue to build. I and many others have been in your shoes wanting to quit their job, but not knowing how to do it.

It is up to you to follow the path that government employees, construction workers, financial analysts, self-employed business owners, and countless others who struggled with working a J.O.B. (Just Over Broke) have already traveled. With me by your side and these lessons as your guide, you will be prepared for what will come your way as you quit.

From a lifetime of learning about business and dreaming of one day quitting my job, I urge you to take that leap of faith and apply these lessons to your exit plan. That leap of faith is having faith in yourself. You can and will be successful in your new life without a job holding you back from what life has in store for you.

This book will help you to make more money from your business and be set up to live the life of your dreams. I will walk you step-by-step through the thought process and show you how to change from fearing a life without a job to being excited to quit your current job. You will learn that there is a right way to quit your job and how you can do it yourself. I promise that if you learn and implement these lessons into your plan, you'll be equipped to be successfully unemployed.

Don't be the person who misses out on opportunities in life because you are stuck in the same dead-end J.O.B. Be the kind of person other people marvel at saying, "I don't know how they do it, but they are living the life of their dreams," the kind of person who sees opportunities in life and takes action immediately.

The lessons contained in this book have been proven to produce long-lasting results. I have already quit my job and you can too! Get ready for a lifetime of happiness without a job, living on your business income, and having enough money to do the things you want to do without being dependent on anyone for a J.O.B. (Just Over Broke) I encourage you to take the first step and start living the life you were meant to live.

Take control of your life right now and make the decision to quit your job and be successfully unemployed.

What You Will Learn

The question comes up quite often in random conversations, "Why don't you have a job?" Each time I get this or some variation of this question, I have to stop myself. I ask them a question in return, "Why do you have a job?" The answers are usually the same, "Because I have bills to pay." As the conversation progresses, what it all boils down to is, they believe the only way to provide for themselves and their families is through a job.

It is not their fault that they have that belief. They have been taught since childhood that this is the way it is supposed to be. We have all been told that we need to go to school to get into a good college, go to a good college to get a good job, get a good job to have a good life, have a good life so you can retire when you are 68 years old and not work again.

What if this way of thinking is completely wrong? What if there was another way to provide for your family without a job? I'm here to tell you that there is another way. Actually, there are MANY ways to live and be successfully unemployed. What you need to do is apply yourself to building a successful business that earns you the amount of income you need to replace the income from your job.

If you picked up this book, you may already understand this concept and have bought into the idea of not having a job. You may already have a "side business" that you want to be able to call your "main business" (more on this later). If you are in this place in your journey, you are on the right track. This book is designed to teach you the lessons you need to know before you quit your job.

It is a scary thing to give up a steady income where the paychecks roll in month after month. If you look at it from another perspective, it should be even more scary giving up your life, week after week, for a regular paycheck. I guarantee you that you will be able to make way more money with your own business than you ever could have with a job working for someone else.

During the months leading up to when I quit, I was very worried about living without a regular paycheck. Looking back now, with the lessons learned and taught in this book, I didn't have anything to fear. I have already successfully quit my job and now live a life unemployed and loving every minute of it. My businesses earn more money than I ever could have earned from my job.

Why You Need this Book

What does it truly mean to be "rich"? The very first definition in the Merriam-Webster Dictionary of the word "rich" is defined as "having abundant possessions and especially material wealth." I can't really argue with that definition. That is seemingly the original definition of the word that we are all taught growing up. This is how most people define the word, but I submit to you that for anyone who wants to be successfully unemployed and independent, "rich" can mean something else.

If you keep going down the list of definitions for the word, you will come to a definition that I believe applies to those who quit their job to be independent and self-sufficient. All the way down to the 7th definition part B, you will read that "rich" is "meaningful" or "significant".

If you are asked who you think is the richest person in the world, you probably think of Bill Gates, Donald Trump, or Warren Buffet. These would definitely fit the first definition of the word. But, would you think of the small business owner that makes hundreds of thousands of dollars a year removing dents from cars? What about the guy that owns the local breakfast house in town who works 2-3 hours a day because he loves talking to his customers? Or, the poker player that does not have a job, but earns his money coaching others to play poker through one-on-one coaching, online courses, webinars, blogs and podcasts? Would you consider these business owners rich?

I submit to you that the term "rich" can also be applied in other ways. It can be applied to those who have the abundance of free time in their lives because they are successfully unemployed. These are the "rich" who can do what they want to do, when they want to do it, and never have to answer to a boss again.

What This Book Is and Is Not

This book is not going to show you "HOW" to quit your job. I am going to assume that you are already going down the entrepreneurial road with your businesses and are making money. Teaching the "HOW" is way beyond the scope of this book. This book is going to teach the lessons you need to know before you quit your job and how to be successfully unemployed.

If you do have questions on how to make money from businesses and passive income, check out my blog, www.masterpassiveincome.com. There is loads of free content on how you can quit your job with many different types of businesses with a special emphasis on passive income. I personally use real estate rental properties to earn enough income to replace the income from my job. This type of business and many others will give you the ability to make enough money each month to replace the income from your regular job.

This book will not tell you to save your money your entire life and retire at age 68 when everyone else retires. This, in itself, is not a bad thing to do and the lessons in this book can apply to those at age 68 as well. The plan laid out in this book is for you to quit your job well before you reach retirement age, and do it successfully.

This book will not help you find your "Dream Job." They say the dream job is doing what you love and being paid for it. I would say that is true for everyone but the entrepreneur who wants to quit their job. Entrepreneurs want to be free of the shackles of a job, even if it is the dream job. With a job, you are still trading your hours for dollars. The best job is one that you do not have to work at all.

What you will learn in this book are the lessons that will help an entrepreneur like yourself with a profitable “side-business” to successfully quit your job and never work another one again. These lessons come from my own personal experiences as well as many others. Think of this book as a road map that is showing you the destination you want to get to.

My goal is to guide you in this journey, to give you the knowledge you need to never work a job again. With these lessons, you will be able to plan your escape from the rat-race of life and finally have the freedom to live your life the way YOU want to.

Take Action

Learning without application is a waste of time and energy. To help you implement these lessons into your plan, there is a "Take Action" section at the end of every lesson for you to apply what you learned.

Once you have built up your businesses to replace your income from your job, you are ready to quit. But if you quit without having a strong plan, thinking through all the hurdles and pitfalls, you may find yourself back working another job. This is not necessarily failure, just a detour. Failure is only when you have given up on your dream to never work a job again.

By planning for the future before you quit, you will be set up for success. For example, if you don't plan for your health insurance before you quit, you may be stuck without it or be paying much more for the insurance than you need to be.

It is always better to be pro-active rather than re-active. If you are re-active in your planning, you are pressed to make quick, and possibly wrong decisions that you would not normally choose to make. You are limited because of the lack of time, money, options, or all the above.

By being pro-active, you have the ability to make much better decisions because you have many more options. Completing each of the "Take Action" sections will help you plan your escape well.

Here's To Your Success!

CHAPTER TWO

MY STORY AND HOW I BECAME SUCCESSFULLY UNEMPLOYED

"The winners in life think constantly in terms of I can, I will, and I am. Losers, on the other hand, concentrate their waking thoughts on what they should have or would have done, or what they can't do."

– Dennis Waitley

The walk down the familiar hallway felt longer than I remembered.

As each footstep hit the ground, I got closer and closer to my boss's office. The doorway of his office looked small from where I was, but it was getting larger and larger as I got closer. As I walked through the hall of the office where I had worked for 9 years, I knew this was the day.

The closer I got, the more I realized that all the rumors were true. Once I arrived at my boss's office, his secretary, a lovely lady, motioned for me to sit down on one of the uncomfortable chairs he had outside his office.

"Have a seat and he will be with you in just a few minutes," she said to me in a soft and reserved manner. Her face was sad and consoling. It was as if I were a lamb being led to the slaughter while she could do nothing to help, but was reserved to just stand there and watch.

Sitting outside of my boss's office, I knew what was about to happen. Minute after minute went by and all I could do was wait. After about five minutes, I heard voices coming from his office as he and another one of my co-workers neared the door for them to exit. The door opened to my co-worker exiting the office with a manila envelope in her hands. This was one of many that were on my boss's desk that he was giving to about 10 employees. I knew that one of those envelopes were for me.

It was 4:30pm on a Friday afternoon. The rumors, signs, hushed conversations, and a meeting with my boss all pointed to one thing.

I was being laid-off.

Little did my boss know... I was ready.

I Had Been Preparing for Something Like This for Many Years

I heard the saying a long time ago: "It's not *if* you lose your job, but *when* you lose your job." As a young college student hearing this, I was obviously concerned about my future. All my life, my schooling had taught me to work hard for someone else. I learned how to be an employee and make the business owner money.

At the young age of 13, like most boys my age, I loved to be active. Playing sports, riding bikes, camping, fishing, and all the other things most boys loved to do. Little did I know that I had a drive in me that others did not have. I had the drive to be independent and self-reliant. Self-motivation was never a problem for me and neither was the ability to buck the system.

My entire life, I found myself questioning all the rules I was given. I had always been "that kid" who questioned and acted against the rules. A good example of this was when I was 3 years old, my Aunt told me not to touch the wall she just painted in her house. Upon hearing the "rule" to not "touch" the paint, I immediately stuck out my hand and planted my entire palm and fingers into that fresh paint. With my entire hand pressed firmly on the new paint, I looked at my aunt in defiance. Needless to say, I received a good spanking for it.

Questioning rules like this seemed easy for me (and painful at times). I found myself innately questioning why things were the way they were. At a young age, I questioned why I needed to work for someone else to make a living. I desired to know how to make money on my own without having a job. This desire probably came because I was told that to earn a living, I needed to go to school and get a good job. It was my ability to look past the rules to see how I can bend, if not break them. Don't get me wrong, I'm not saying break the laws, breaking the law is a crime and should not be done. I am talking about those rules that others impose on you because they impose it on themselves.

There is one "rule" that I am very glad I broke many years ago. The "rule" is: Go to school, go to college, get a job, save money, buy a home, get out of debt, invest in the stock market, work until the "government designated" retirement age of 68 to retire, then live on your savings and hope it doesn't run out.

This "rule" seemed ridiculous to me as a young adult. Why wait until 68 to retire? Why do I need to work for someone else my entire life, making them money while I work my life away? I decided to break this "rule" because I did not want to wait 50 years to not have a job. My rationale was that someone needed to be the business owner, but why did it have to be someone else? If someone had to be the business owner, why couldn't it be me?

How I Successfully Quit My Job

The adrenaline pumped through my veins.

Looking at the flickering neon Coca Cola sign in the retail business I started 6 months prior, I envisioned my not-so-distant future ahead of me. A future where I would never have to work for anyone ever again. I had just gotten back from an on-site visit to Youngstown Ohio where I had recently put in an offer for an investment home for $17,000 in cash.

"Okay Dustin, the property is yours," Dave, my seasoned Realtor informed me over the phone from Ohio. Even though I was living in California, I saw the potential of real estate in other areas of the country and bought another rental property there. My goal was not to flip houses, but to own and rent them.

"Terrific, thanks Dave! Please give the keys to my property manager so she can get the place rented." I replied with a little anxiety in my voice. It took a lot of convincing for my wife to agree to spend our life savings on an investment property 3000 miles away. My sales pitch to her was that we would earn passive income in monthly cash flow by renting the house to tenants we would never meet.

Since this was the first investment property we had ever bought, it was quite the nerve racking experience, filled with uncertainty and doubt.

The following questions came to my mind:

- Did I do the right thing with our life savings?
- Was this the right house to buy for an investment?
- Was this the right area to invest in?
- What if the house caught fire and burnt down?

- What would we do if we get horrible tenants?
- What will we do if the furnace goes out and there is a $2500 expense?
- How do we manage a rental property when we have never done it before?

After hanging up the phone with my realtor, all these questions and more swirled inside my head. For some reason, though, maybe it is the optimist in me, I knew everything would be just fine. Looking back now, everything has been just fine, as long as we kept the course of building businesses with passive income.

For the next nine years, every penny I earned from the passive income went back into the business to make more passive income. Year after year, I bought more and more properties. Each property brought in more money that I would then use to buy more properties.

Here is the timeline for how I bought my first 19 properties:

- July 2007: Property 1
    - Cash price $17,000 – Rents for $525
    - Refinanced the property and took out $15,000 to buy my second property.
- October 2007: Property 2
    - Cash price $10,200 – Rents for $550
    - Refinanced the property and took out $20,000 to buy two more properties.
- April 2008: Property 3
    - Cash price $10,000 – Rents for $500
- June 2008: Property 4
    - Cash price $7,500 – Rents for $500

In real estate, buying properties with creative financing is one strategy to grow the business fast. One creative way to get financing is to use a credit card to purchase a property. You may say to me, "That is crazy risky!" Sure, it would be crazy if you were getting a 21% interest rate on the loan! It would also be crazy if you didn't know what you were doing.

The credit card I took advantage of was a cash out offer of 1.50% interest rate for the life of the loan. Think about it. A regular loan would be at least 4% interest for the life of the loan. With this credit card, I would only be paying 1.5%! Even with the different way credit cards calculate interest, this was a huge win!

With a credit limit of $14,000, I pulled out every penny I could to purchase the next property. This next property brought in $525 a month in rent. Since the interest on the credit was only $50 a month, I was ahead $475! Talk about a great loan!

- September 2008: Property 5
    - Cash price $13,000 – Rents for $525
- September 2008: Property 6
    - Cash price $6,500 – Rents for $500
- October 2008: Property 7
    - Cash price $6,500 – Rents for $500
- March 2010: Property 8
    - Cash price $7,800 – Rents for $500
- July 2010: Property 9
    - Cash price $9,200 – Rents for $525
- May 2011: Property 10
    - Cash price $10,500 – Rents for $525
- June 2011: Property 11
    - Cash price $9,000 – Rents for $500

- July 2011: Property 12 & 13 (Duplex)
    - Cash price $12,000 – Rents for $850
- February 2012: Property 14
    - Cash price $8,900 – Rents for $525
- April 2013: Property 15
    - Cash price $11,000 – Rents for $525
- February 2013: Property 16
    - Cash price $7,800 – Rents for $525
- March 2013: Property 17
    - Cash price $8,200 – Rents for $495
- December 2013: Property 18
    - Cash price $8,900 – Rents for $525
- November 2015: Property 19
    - Cash price $9,000 – Rents for $495

The total rental income, not including expenses, for these properties each month is: $9,590! Not too bad for 8 years of investing! Building up a business that has 19 properties took hard work, sacrifice, and dedication.

Disclaimer!

I must say that the business model for investing in rental property business is very complex. I will not go into detail on how to effectively run this type of business because it would be way out of the scope of this book. If you want more detail on these, I have much more information on how to invest in rental properties on my blog www.masterpassiveincome.com. There, you will find blog posts, online courses, books, and other resources on how you can quit your job with these passive income ideas.

Since 2015, I have continued to build my rental business to even more properties and passive income in the form of monthly cash flow. Each property I buy brings in more money for me to buy more properties, which brings in more money so I can buy more properties and so on. I will probably never stop buying properties.

In December 2016, I worked my last day at a job ever. Because I pushed hard for 9 years, I am blessed to have quit my job and never have to work again.

Resignation Day

It was a red painted lobster on a white canvas. As I sat there looking at this painting, I couldn't help but feel all the emotion of 9 years of work wash over me.

As simple as it was, this piece of art always stirred something in me that made me strive every day to build my businesses so I could quit my job. Going through the images, pictures, and paintings on my cubicle wall, my eyes found this painting again and I had to pause for a moment.

It caused a flood of memories and emotions to come over me. After a moment of reflection, I got choked up thinking this would be the first day of the rest of my life. Because of that painting, I set in motion all those years ago a plan to never have to work a job again. Even though I landed a great job in another county department after I was laid off from my original job, I still wanted out.

Reaching for that hand (and foot) painted picture of a red lobster to take it off the wall marked the culmination of 9 years of hard work and dedication. This piece of artwork had been hanging on the wall of my cubicle at my job since my oldest daughter painted it when she was only one year old. Obviously, she had help from a volunteer in her Sunday school class at church, but it was made by her.

One upside-down foot made the body, two hands made the claws, and red paint made up the lobster. At first glance, I couldn't tell what it was, but my imagination took over and now I see that beautiful lobster painted by my daughter with her tiny hands and feet.

The reason why I desired to quit my job was to be with my wife and children more and work less. The picture my first child painted was the inspiration and motivation to keep pushing, keep building and never stop my plan to quit my job with passive income.

This was the day I officially resigned from my job working as a Systems and Procedures Analyst for the County government. It was a great job. If I had no ambition to be on my own, this was the perfect job.

- Earned over $78,000 a year
- Worked 4 days a week at 10 hours a day with 3 days off every week
- Received 90% of my pay as pension when I retired
- Earned 11.5 hours of vacation time every two weeks
- Was able to do 40 hours of work in only 10 hours
- Enjoyable coworkers to work with (for the most part)

Even with all these benefits, I desired more for my life. My desire was to get paid for the value that I brought, not the hours that I worked. I personally hate trading dollars for hours. That is, getting paid an hourly wage for one hour of work. If I did not work, I did not get paid.

This day, my resignation day, was the start of the rest of my life. Being only 37 when I quit my job, I still had half of my life to live outside of having a job. For me, working until I was 68 years old would have been an absolute loss for me. That would be another 31 years of working for someone else, rather than myself, again, a loss.

The walk to my car after work on December 15th 2016 was the best walk I ever took. As I left my job for the final time, with all my family pictures, including that red lobster, and personal items in tow, I couldn't help but think that I was very blessed.

That was the first day of the rest of my life. Now I can do

whatever I want, whenever I want, and never answer to a boss again!

You know, on that beautiful rainy walk to my car, I couldn't help but think how all this was possible. Looking back over the past 9 years of my life building my passive income businesses, it was all worth it. All the sacrifices, hard times, ups-and-downs of the passive income business life was absolutely worth it. I am proof that this passive income thing really works!

At age 37, I quit my job and will NEVER work a job again! And this is all thanks to passive income and the businesses I have created.

This day was the first day of the rest of my life!

Life After A Job = Amazing!

Now, far removed from my job, I am living the life most people only dream about.

- Earning money each month from my businesses
- Going on a six-week trip to Japan
- Snow skiing 3-4 days a week
- Deer hunting for weeks on end
- Working 3 hours a month on my rental business
- Making thousands each month from my online businesses
- Doing whatever I want to do.

The first thing I did after I quit my job was go on a six-week vacation to Japan with my family. The six of us, with my father, traveled all over the country sight-seeing everything there was to be seen, ate the best sushi, enjoyed Tokyo Disneyland and Disney Sea, ate the best Kobe Beef in Kobe Japan, did CrossFit in a Tokyo box (gym), stayed in the best places, all while still making money from my businesses. Each business makes money without me doing any work of my own and I only work when I want to.

Some people asked, "Why would you spend such a long time in Japan, six weeks is a long time." My reply to them is, "Because I can." I don't have a job to get back to, my businesses run themselves, what little work I need to do I can do with my laptop and a Wi-Fi connection and a cup of green tea.

The second thing I did was move my family from California to Arizona to be closer to my wife's side of the family. I didn't need to find a job, I didn't need a job. I could actually live anywhere in the world I desired. I am not anchored down to a physical location because of a job. Again, my computer and a Wi-Fi connection are all that I need to run my business.

Next, I took my family on many mini-vacations around California. Carmel-by-the-Sea, Monterey Bay Aquarium, South Lake Tahoe, Pismo Beach, Yosemite, all were amazing trips that we thoroughly enjoyed.

The last thing I did was... nothing. Absolutely nothing at all. Why? Because I could.

Life without a job is absolutely amazing when you are prepared and are successfully unemployed because you planned your escape from your job well in advance.

CHAPTER THREE

R.I.C.H. WILL CHANGE YOUR LIFE

"Whatever the mind of man can conceive and believe, it can achieve. Thoughts are things! And powerful things at that, when mixed with definiteness of purpose, and burning desire, can be translated into riches."

– Napoleon Hill

R.I.C.H. is your new acronym for your way of life and how you can prepare for life after you quit your job. The **RICH** lessons you are going to learn in this book are from someone who has already quit his job and blazed the trail for you to follow.

The sections in this book will help you create a plan for you to quit your job and be set up to be successfully unemployed. I encourage you to learn and apply these lessons before you jump into being a full-time Entrepreneur and never work for anyone ever again.

R is for Realization of Self-Worth

You are worth more than the paycheck you receive every two weeks. The value that you bring to your business is worth much more than any amount of money you can make per hour. All you need to do is realize that when your employer is paying you for your hour, he is really paying you to do something that will make him more money.

Why not employ yourself and make 100% of the money from the time you spend working? Why shouldn't it be YOU who profits from your hard work and life spent building something? I'm telling you that there is no reason why YOU couldn't be the business owner, the investor, or the entrepreneur who makes money from your time spent doing work on your own business.

It is time for you to realize you are worth more than your hourly wage.

I is for an Independent Attitude

Your independence is invaluable. Think of your independence as freedom. Would you not pay all the money you had for your freedom? Slavery have been around for thousands of years and did not start in America. Just about every slave desired their freedom. They would dream of the ability to work hard every day to buy their freedom. Think about that for a minute. BUY YOUR FREEDOM.

In today's world, we have all been lulled to sleep in our lives. We have been taught from a very young age that we all must go to school, then go to college, then get a good job and then work until retirement. This is no longer slavery where someone forces you to work, but is a sort of self-inflicted slavery. Slavery to the job you work day-in and day-out. This is nowhere near as horrible as actual slavery. It does, however, have the same outcome. You work for someone so they can profit from your time and life.

It's time to challenge that way of thinking, time to have an independent attitude, and time to work hard to gain your freedom.

C is for Capital Growth

To live a life free from a job, you need to be successfully unemployed. The income that you receive from your businesses must replace the income from your job. So, you need to properly prepare for the time your paycheck stops coming in.

Sustaining, growing, and multiplying your income is the key to this section of your planning. Without having 40 hours of your life taken up each week by a job, you can spend those 40 hours making more money for you and your family by growing your capital.

H is for Hacking Your Future

There are many benefits that come with your job. Honestly, you don't need them. They are nice to have, but you do not NEED them. By being successfully unemployed, you will plan your way around these benefits to having a job. Your new businesses will match these benefits AND even surpass them.

Your future must be hacked because the system is made for you to work a job. By successfully hacking your future, you will be ready for all that life will throw at you. You will see things coming way in advance and be prepared for them, and even laugh at them.

Being "**RICH**" is no longer just for those who were idolized on the 80's TV show "Lifestyles of the Rich and Famous". Those lavish lifestyles with million dollar yachts, ridiculously huge mansions, and private planes. Yes, these are not bad in and of themselves, but the new definition of "Rich" is all about the ability to design your life how YOU want it. If you want the yacht, mansion, and private plane, it is up to you to build a business that will accommodate that lifestyle.

Being "**RICH**" is about lifestyle design and living your life without a job the way YOU want to live. With this new thinking of what rich can be for you, these lessons will help you to have a different perspective about your future without a job.

Section 1

R is for Realization of Self-Worth

"Every great dream begins with a dreamer. Always remember, you have within you the strength, the patience, and the passion to reach for the stars to change the world."

- Harriet Tubman

You are worth more money than an hourly wage that you could earn from any job.

I know that sounds crazy to hear but it's true. Since elementary school, we have all been trained to work day-in and day-out at a job to make money to support ourselves. The reality is that you can make so much more money on your own than you ever could working for someone else. No matter what job you have, or how much you make per hour, you are worth much more than that.

If you really think about it, the hourly wage you are paid shows how much our employer believes we are worth. If you have a minimum wage job, you are only worth that to your employer. If your hourly wage is $100 an hour, then that is exactly how much you are worth. I'm here to tell you that you are worth much more than ANYONE can pay you. What you are being paid is not a true reflection of what you are worth.

Your time should not be valued in dollars and cents. What you are worth is the value that you bring to anything that you do and whatever you apply yourself to. When you accept an hourly wage, you are agreeing with your employer on how much your time and talents are worth.

Let's look at this in a different way. You are worth what you bring to the table, so to speak. If you are paid for the value you bring, you would be making money from what you produce with your time. This is drastically different than being paid in the form of an hourly wage. You inherently know that you are worth more than you are getting paid at your job right now. It is time for you to understand just how much you are worth. Your worth is based on what **YOU** believe you are worth, not what someone else believes you are worth.

Having a realization of your self-worth comes when you look at how your life is being spent. You are the valuable commodity, not your job. There are millions of jobs in the world, but there is only one you. If you settle for a job, any job, you are limiting yourself. Once you realize your job is holding you back from your true potential, your only limit is the one that you place upon yourself.

YOUR WORTH IS BASED ON WHAT YOU BELIEVE YOU ARE WORTH, NOT WHAT SOMEONE ELSE BELIEVES YOU ARE WORTH.

For section 1, **R is for Realization of Self-Worth**. Once you realize your self-worth, the sky's the limit for you. I will say it again; you are worth more money than any job can pay you. That statement is true. Now, all you need to think about is how much money you will make without a job and how your business will prove that.

CHAPTER FOUR

LESSON 1

HOW TO BE THE RICHEST PERSON IN THE WORLD

"Beauty is in the eye of the beholder."

- Margaret Wolfe Hungerford

I couldn't help but laugh.

"I didn't know you were that rich." Matt, a friend of mine said to me one day.

"What?" I replied

"You are quitting your job, you have to be rich!" He added.

"I'm not rich," I said as I chuckled a bit.

"You don't have to be rich to quit your job," I said. I paused to read the expression on his face.

"You just need to make enough passive income to replace your earned income."

He looked a little puzzled as the thought of my quitting quickly sank in.

"No," I continued. "I am not rich but I have all my needs met with my rental properties and online businesses that I do not need to work. It has taken me nine years to get to this point and I am ready to quit."

"What do you mean you have all your needs met?" he asked.

"Well, my businesses bring in money in the form of cash flow each month. That means that each month, I have money put into my pocket from my businesses. I have built up my businesses enough that the income each month has surpassed the income from my job."

"So, your rental properties bring in rent and your online businesses bring in money from advertising and sales?" he asked as he was starting to understand.

"Correct! There are ups and downs in sales and rent amount each month but on average, all my expenses are paid for by my businesses. I am quitting my job, not because I'm rich, but because I can," I said.

As we sat in the waiting room of a large hospital to see my best friend who was fighting for his life, I went further into detail on two things; the "How" and the "Why" of me quitting my job. You see, he believed that only rich people did not have jobs. Well, I guess if that is the definition of being rich, then I am truly rich.

Some people desire to have expensive cars, fancy homes and a lavish lifestyle. Those things are fine for some, but that is not what I desired when I made the commitment to myself to quit my job. I wanted the ability to no longer work for someone else and spend more time with my amazing wife and beautiful children. I also wanted to have the freedom to do the things I wanted to do. So, yes, I most definitely am rich by those standards and I agree. Honestly, this is what my entire goal was 9 years prior, to be independent and not have to work for anyone.

What I explained to Matt was that the "Why" was just as important as the "How" in anything and especially when it came to quitting your job. If you don't know why you desire to quit your job, how will you know when it is the right time to quit? Some people make money their passion. The end goal is the money itself. The problem with having money be your passion is that you get to become just like J.D. Rockefeller, one of the richest men in history.

When he was asked the question "How much money is enough?" his answer was very telling of his passion for money, "Just a little bit more." The desire for money never stops, but can actually become your master if you let it. As you pursue it, it will always flee from you.

I find it is best to use it as a tool for the more important things in life. On my death bed, I would regret the time I wasted chasing after things that were not important. What is important is my Lord, my wife, my children, my family, and my friends. Everything else is not important. Reminds me of a quote from a movie I rather enjoy called "The Fifth Element" starring Bruce Willis and Chris Tucker.

I WANTED THE ABILITY TO NO LONGER WORK FOR SOMEONE ELSE AND SPEND MORE TIME WITH MY FAMILY WHILE DOING THE THINGS I WANT TO DO.

When told, there was "no time" to go a course of action, the priest responded, "Time is of no importance, only life is important." As Matt and I sat patiently in the waiting room of the large hospital, it was easy for him to see that life was short. It can be taken away from us at any moment. No one is guaranteed to be alive tomorrow.

As I explained this to Matt, he began to understand that you don't need millions of dollars to quit your job. I, on the other hand, realized that I actually was rich. But, not in the way most people might think. I can't, and wouldn't if I could, go out and buy a Ferrari, Lamborghini or some other expensive toy. No, I am rich in a different sense of the word. I am rich in time and life, not money.

Life is the most expensive thing you can spend. Your time, which equates to your life, is much more valuable than money. Even though I have enough money to never work a job again, I actually have the rest of my life to live my own way.

Yes, being able to quit your job and doing the things you want to do will make you feel like you are the richest person in the world. For some, this may not be enough. Since beauty is in the eye of the beholder, the only perspective that matters is mine, not someone else's perspective or opinion.

The day I quit my job, I felt like the richest person in the world.

Do You Want To Be Rich?

"Do you want to be so rich and have so much money that you don't know what to do with it?!" Joey said with excitement!

He was the instructor of the free, 1-hour real estate investment class/sales pitch. He was there on behalf of a real estate "guru" who recently had many infomercials playing on late night TV in my area.

"Do you want to be so rich that you can travel the world the rest of your life? Or can buy a luxury car, or even buy a vacation home in Hawaii?" He continued.

The excitement in the room from the attendees was almost palpable.

"No," I answered to myself. Not sure why I was answering his question this way, but found myself really contemplating the question.

As I listened to the entire real estate "course" from the instructor, all I could think about was being able to quit my job and never work for someone again. My answer to his question again was "no". Crazy as it sounds, I really only wanted independence from everyone. The thought that I could work for myself, make my own schedule, have unlimited income, and actually "make" money rather than "earn" money got me passionate about real estate and passive income.

All those things the instructor mentioned would be nice, but I wanted freedom. Financial, physical and emotional freedom from what comes with having a job. A job that tied me down and kept me from living the life I wanted to live, whatever that life looked like. I wanted to be independent and free to do whatever I wanted without the hindrance of a job.

Throughout the instructor's hour long free "course", I kept reminding myself "Independence is freedom, freedom is independence."

Being dependent on a job has the feeling of wearing the type of shackles that an inmate would wear in a prison. Those shackles will only allow the wearer to go where the jailer allows him to go. A job is the shackles that an employer uses to keep his employee doing what he wants him to do.

THE THOUGHT THAT I COULD WORK FOR MYSELF, MAKE MY OWN SCHEDULE, HAVE UNLIMITED INCOME, AND ACTUALLY "MAKE" MONEY RATHER THAN "EARN" MONEY GOT ME PASSIONATE ABOUT REAL ESTATE AND PASSIVE INCOME.

Wearing these shackles makes one beholden to their boss, his boss's boss, and his boss's boss. The fear of losing our entire income that we depend on to provide for our family comes from the inevitability of us being released from the job we depend on.

While the instructor gave little tidbits of information about how to be rich, it seemed as though I was the only one who was not jumping out of my seat by what the instructor was saying. Maybe it is the skeptic in me, but I knew there was a catch. As the instructor went on, I realized that all this was just a big sales pitch for something that was going to cost more money.

"If you want to become filthy rich, all you need to do is to pay $1000 for you and a friend to come to our two-day seminar on the things I shared today." The instructor was closing the deal.

There it was. A sales pitch for $1000 to come out of my pocket for something that seemed to be attainable. The thought of being able to quit my job with passive income in real estate was fascinating. Being a 27-year-old wannabe entrepreneur and ready to quit my job after 4 years working there, I was ready. The new world of passive income in real estate rental properties was just opened to me and I knew I had a lot to learn. With the help of my step-dad, we both attended the two-day seminar together.

The seminar was actually very good and opened my eyes to the possibility of making passive income from rental properties. That passive income would help me quit my job because of the cash flow coming in on a monthly basis. There it was, the light at the end of the tunnel was dim, but at least I could see it. ***A life without a job.***

Find Your "Why" for Your Life

Now that I shared with you my "why" for quitting my job, it is time for you to find your "why." This step is more important than you possibly realize. Having a why that drives you to succeed at times may be the only thing keeping you going when things get really hard.

Think about these things as you consider your "Why" for you to quit your job.

What excites you?

There must be something that you desire to do in life that would take the place of your work. Something that you can't stop thinking about or even keeps you up at night. If your desire is to be a full-time lead guitarist for a band, nothing could stop you from practicing, playing with friends, learning new songs, and finding a band to play with.

Your "Why" could even be something that possibly keeps you up at night. Maybe it is being a professional golfer? All your time and thoughts go to how to improve your game, finding new ways to put spin on the ball or even practicing your putting at night while you watch TV.

Think of the things that excite you and write them down. Narrow the list to one or at most two and spend a few days thinking about each. Having more than one is not an issue, but not having one at all, is an issue.

What are your strengths?

Each of us has different strengths and weaknesses. Focus on your strengths and how they can help you get to your goal? Another way to think of it would be, "what are you good at"?

The answer to this question should be applied to the first question. Your strengths should coincide with what gets you excited. You were created with a unique set of abilities and talents that work with your desires. As you focus on your strengths, the things you are excited about will become more pronounced and prominent.

For example, my strengths are managing many things at one time. Real Estate investing has many moving parts and having the ability to manage everything well is a must. There are many people to manage, lead, and develop in the business that others may hate doing. I personally love this about real estate investing and feel more alive when I am working on my business.

Play to your strengths and they will help you fulfill your "Why" and help you to achieve your goals.

TAKE ACTION

Name three "Why's" that are driving you to quit your job. List them in order here:

1. ____

2. ____

3. ____

What are three strengths you have that will help you build your business? List them here:

1. ____

2. ____

3. ____

What does success look like to you? What can you accomplish to make yourself feel as though you are the richest person in the world? Write your response below:

____

____

____

____

____

____

CHAPTER FIVE

LESSON 2

LEARN HOW TO BE AN ENTREPRENEUR

"Being an entrepreneur isn't just a job title, and it isn't just about starting a company. It is a state of mind. It's about seeing connections others can't, seizing opportunities others won't, and forging new directions that others haven't."

- Tory Burch

My jaw almost hit the floor.

"And the next level of training is a 2 week long intensive training in our Florida offices where we will walk you, step-by-step through the process of finding your first property. It will only cost $25,000, not including your travel and living costs." The apprentice of the real estate "guru" said in my two-day seminar.

"What?!" I thought to myself.

Thoughts raced through my mind about having to pay someone $25,000 to show me how to make money. I didn't even have $2,500 to my name let alone $25,000. This was probably why at the end of the first day of the seminar, they gave us the steps to "increase" our credit score.

We were instructed to call each of our credit card companies and request the largest amount of an increase in credit we could get. The student with the highest dollar increase would win a prize. I guess they didn't care if people went into debt, as long as they got their money.

Could this be what I needed to do in order to gain my financial freedom? Spend $25,000 for more "hands on" training? In my mind, if I was not smart enough to be successful on what they taught me in the 2-day seminar, the 2-week seminar wouldn't help much.

"No thank you," I said to the team of salesmen ready to take my money.

The Key Trait for Any Entrepreneur

Entrepreneurs need to be just like Vanilla Ice. "If there was a problem, Yo, I'll solve it." I know it's a bit corny, but I think you get the point. Being an entrepreneur is basically being a problem solver. When you really think about it, every business is basically solving a problem.

BEING A PROBLEM SOLVER IS VITAL TO BEING AN ENTREPRENEUR.

Just think of the auto industry and why automobiles were invented. They were invented because the horse and buggy was slower and an animal dependent form of transportation. The horse and buggy was invented to help people move from place to place faster than walking. The whole problem that was solved was transportation in a fast, efficient, and convenient way.

Likewise, think of your local grocery store where you buy your food. If you boil it down, the problem was where to get food. Rather than planting and growing your crops, raising your own cattle, or hunting for your food, you could go to one place to buy everything you needed.

Being a problem solver is vital to being an entrepreneur. Every day, I get a problem to solve in my businesses. Whether it is a furnace that goes out in one of my properties, how to finance a new property that I am buying, or how to fix a problem on my website, these are all problems that I need to solve.

As a problem solver, I found that the two-week seminar would be a problem for me because I did not have the money to take the course, but still needed to learn the information that was provided. This problem was easily solved by reading real estate investment books, watching online videos, and even reading blogs on how to do real estate investing.

No matter what the problem is, an entrepreneur will always find a way.

Your business is different than your job

The chair he was sitting in was much larger than it needed to be. Chuck, the Business Administrator of the church I was attending at the time was an older man, in his late 70's, and was a very accomplished businessman. He had owned many businesses. He not only didn't need the business administrator job, I believe he actually did it for free.

As I entered into his office to discuss some ministry business, he started the conversation with a question.

"How's your business doing?" He said with curiosity.

"My work is going fine. My boss thinks I'm doing a good job and I just got a raise," I replied.

"No, not your job, how is your business? Your job is your job. This is fine, but I am curious about your business. How is that going," he said.

He knew that I had a small graphic and website design company that serviced many small customers in the area. After I considered his question for a moment, I realized that I had made a huge mistake. Even though I knew I wanted to be out of my job and be an entrepreneur, I still considered myself an employee. My first reaction to his question was how my job was going because I considered myself to be an employee with a side business.

YOU ARE NO LONGER AN EMPLOYEE WITH A SIDE BUSINESS, BUT AN ENTREPRENEUR WITH A SIDE JOB.

How you see yourself is how others will see you. If you see yourself as an employee, that is what they will see you as. If you see yourself as a business owner, that is how others will see you. I was projecting myself still as an employee even though I had my small business for 5 years and was doing quite well. In response to his question, I should have considered myself as an entrepreneur business owner with a side job.

The first time I began telling people that I was a real estate investor was very nerve-racking for me. Even though I already had over a dozen properties, I felt as though my identity was still with my job.

A common question most people get is "So, what do you do for living?" The easiest answer is where you are employed. For an entrepreneur, this is what you should not say. When you are asked this question, you need to identify yourself as the business owner you are and what type of business you run.

You are no longer an employee with a side business, but an entrepreneur with a side job. Even if you just started your business five days ago, you are a business owner and need to picture yourself as one.

You may even feel as though you are an impostor posing as a business owner, don't let that stop you from picturing yourself as one.

The more you tell yourself that you are a business owner, the more you will believe it and the more others will believe it. If all else fails, fake it until you make it. Trust me, the longer you see yourself as a business owner, the easier it will be.

Learn, Learn, Learn. Never Stop Learning

My forehead was dripping with sweat again.

"Mr. Heiner, your seat is right over here. When you are ready, click the start button on the test and begin. You will have four hours to complete the test. Please report back to me when you are done," the Proctor said in a monotone voice that would make you fall asleep.

"Thank you," I said nervously as I took my seat and got ready to take the four-hour test. As I positioned the mouse over the start button for the test, I couldn't help but think how much I hated taking tests. They always felt to me like they were not a true representation of my knowledge or abilities. It also didn't help that I was a horrible test-taker and always second-guessed my answers.

It was the third time I had taken the Graduate Management Admissions Test (GMAT). It is the SAT's for business schools. At 22 years old, I thought the only way I could succeed in business would be by getting a Masters of Business Administration (MBA) at a prestigious school. The first two times I took the GMAT, my scores were horrible. Out of 800 total points, my best score was 522. In order to get into any good business school, I would need to at least get 700.

After applying to business college and realizing that my test scores were not good enough, evidenced in fact by my rejection letters, I decided I needed to get my education elsewhere. Maybe it was just me, but I felt as though my college education was a waste of time and money. Even though I studied business and entrepreneurship in college, I felt I only learned what other people wanted me to learn.

Classes like Accounting 4A & 4B were a complete waste of time for me. I hate accounting with a passion. Even though I understand numbers in business, it is definitely not something I have a desire to do or learn more about. I was even forced to take classes that had nothing to do with business as a part of my education to get a regular bachelor's degree. For some people, these classes are fine to take. But for me, it was a huge waste of time and money. After all my education, I have realized that I only want to learn what I want to learn, not what someone else tells me to learn.

As an entrepreneur, I play to my strengths and pay other people to do the things either I am not good at or do not want to do. Since I hate accounting, I pay my accountant to crunch all the numbers and do my taxes. I also hate property management and dealing with tenants, so I pay my property manager to do the work for me. I also hate designing covers for my books and formatting the pages so I pay a designer to do it.

There is, however, something that entrepreneurs just can't outsource or get around. That one thing is learning. As much as I never want to go to school again, I know that I will always need to learn new things that will help my business succeed. Just because I never want to go to school again doesn't mean that I never want to learn anything again. In fact, it is just the opposite.

The further removed I am from school, the more I realize how much I don't know and how much I need to learn about my business and how to make it better. Learning how to be a better business owner and how to refine your tradecraft is vital for any entrepreneur or business owner. The day a business owner feels that they know everything and do not need to learn anymore is the day their business begins to die.

It is said that "leaders are readers." I fully agree with that. I personally try to read or listen to as many books or audio books as I can. I then apply it to my business and life. I find that the more books I read, the better I become and the more money I can make. It is good to learn from your mistakes, but why not learn from other people's mistakes and never make them yourself? As you learn and read about how others perform in business and life, you will have learned from years of other's life experiences and can apply them to yourself.

To quote one of my favorite movies "Tommy Boy" with the late Chris Farley and David Spade; when talking about his business, Tommy's dad said, "Ron, don't tell me the bank thinks we need to wait it out. Any business that tries to wait it out is just that, out. In auto-parts, you're either growing or you're dying. There ain't no third direction."

The same goes with every business and every entrepreneur: you are either growing or dying, there ain't no third direction. Entrepreneurs must continually be learning new ways to make their business better, make more money from their existing business, and find new ways to make money. There will always be a competitor who will take over your place in line for your customer's money.

You do not always have to go to school. You do not have to go to a big-name school to learn how to be successful in business. You just need to learn how your business can become better, stronger, faster, and make more money.

Never stop learning.

Find A Mentor

"Do or do not, there is no try." – Master Yoda (Star Wars)

I never understood, and still don't, why people pay money to "life coaches." Apparently, a life coach is someone who will help you see what you are doing wrong and tell you how to make your life better. This seems rather funny to me because anyone can call himself a life coach and market himself to the masses.

I have personally known a few people who try to make money as a "life coach" giving out their "wisdom" to anyone who will pay them, or just listen. The sad thing is that if you really know the person, who they are, how they treat people, and how they run their business, you would never pay them a dime because they don't even practice what they preach. Even worse, they make you believe that they are already successful and in a place where you want to be.

There were two great movies that came out many years ago, one movie had an old man helping a young man learn to defend himself, and the other had a three-foot-tall, 900-year-old green alien with long pointy ears teaching a different young man how to defend himself as well. In both cases, the young men were students of the older mentor who taught them what they knew.

Of course, these two movies are "The Karate Kid" and "Star Wars." If you haven't seen either of these two movies, I highly recommend that you do. However, the point is twofold: 1) a student who wants to learn something needs a mentor and 2) every mentor needs to be found by the student.

Imagine Yoda advertising on Facebook his life coaching ability to teach people how to use the force to defend themselves. Try to picture Mr. Miyagi going to competitions with advertising flyers of his life coaching ability and how he can teach young kids to defend themselves from big bullies. What we see in both movies is that the student sought out the mentor who was already where the student wanted to be in life and was willing to devote all his time to learn how to become like his mentor.

Could Luke Skywalker and Daniel-san have learned on their own how to defend themselves? Maybe. It would have taken them much longer to develop their skills without the help of their mentor. Without Mr. Miyagi, Daniel-san would have gone the entire school year being beat up by his enemies rather than winning the Karate tournament and getting the girl in just one month. I use these two movies to illustrate the point that having a mentor who already is where you want to be, is the best option to show you the path to get there.

A Map Will Show the Path Others Have Already Taken

Imagine yourself going on a trip to Disney World in Orlando, Florida. Without a map showing you the direction to get there, it would take you months to finally get to see Mickey face-to-face. With a map, one that shows you the shortest route, places you can stop along the way, and even possible dangers that may come in your path to the Magic Kingdom, you will get there in the most efficient manner and the shortest time possible.

Think of a mentor as someone who has already arrived in a place where you want to be. They already took the path, they know where to go, what to avoid, and they have made a map for you to get there. The mentor will also guide you along the way if you get tripped up, have questions or just need encouragement to keep going. No matter who your mentor is, he or she should be in the place that you want to be.

The best way to find a mentor is to search for them. Just like Luke Skywalker searched for Yoda who did not necessarily want to be found, Luke went to where Yoda was. If your goal is to run a marathon, then cycle a 100-mile race and compete in an Iron-Man triathlon race, you need to seek out someone who has already done that and go to where they are. If your goal is to be the best real estate agent in your town, you ask everyone you know in the business who is the most successful real estate agent in town. Once you find that person, it is now your job to sell yourself as a potential student.

The best mentors are those who are already where you want to be and have a desire to share their experiences because they have a passion for helping people. You will find that most successful people are willing to share their experiences with you if you just buy them a cup of coffee. In order to get a mentor though, you need to show your potential mentor how you can be of benefit to them.

What you are asking for in a mentor is their time. To them, their time is the most precious thing they have and they're not going to just give it to you for free. It is on you to figure out how you can be of benefit to them in a way that will help them as well. If it is just a one-way relationship where you are taking but not giving back, the potential mentor would probably desire to spend his time doing other things, rather than teaching you.

I have personally helped many people get to be where I am. One particular student of mine went from owning no investment properties to four in one year, making an extra $1800 in passive income each month. What he needed was a road-map to get to where I am as well as the ability to ask questions along the way. Where I had a 10-year plan to quit my job he has a four-year plan to quit his.

He and I talked four years prior about the potential of investing in rental properties and how I was on my way to quit my job. He understood the benefits and desired to get started, but never actually did. Now, four years later, he is on his way to quit his job with rental property business. If he would have started four years ago when we first talked, he could possibly already have quit his job by now.

TAKE ACTION

What are the two major problems you are faced with that is hindering you from quitting your job? List them here:

1. ____

2. ____

Brainstorm solutions to these problems. Write down your ideas below:

____

____

____

____

____

____

____

Who can you look to as a mentor for your business? List three people you will ask to be a mentor.

Possible Mentor 1: ____

Possible Mentor 2: ____

Possible Mentor 3: ____

Give yourself no more than 1 week to reach out to them. Offer to help them with their business in any way in order to learn from them and be mentored by them.

CHAPTER SIX

LESSON 3

THE DRIVE OF AN ENTREPRENEUR

"I actually think being an entrepreneur Is a state of mind. If you're going to be an entrepreneur, my thesis is that you have to sacrifice everything for some period in your life to be successful, refocused and unbalanced in every way. Once you achieve success, you're free to do whatever you like."

– Kevin O'Leary

His apartment sized bird cage was full of hundreds, if not thousands of birds.

I watched in amazement as Sam filled box after box with birds for his business. It was 3:30am and he was plucking the birds out of the air, effortlessly placing them into boxes to be sold in the next couple hours.

He looked as though he was focused, intent, purposeful, and having the time of his life. Even though it was 3:30 in the morning, Sam was alive.

Just a few years before, Sam quit his good paying job to live his life the way he wanted. He did not want to be tied down to a 40+ hour a week job. Because of Sam's businesses and passive income, he only works one day a week. At 2:30am, he wakes up on a Friday morning to take his weekly trip to Los Angeles from Fresno selling birds to big box stores, little stores, and even swap-meet vendors.

On the one day of the week he works, he works hard. The 10-hour round trip from Fresno to LA is a ride he takes with joy as he sells his birds along this stretch of California Highway 5. Before he started his business selling birds, Sam worked for UPS as a truck loader and then driver. The problem for Sam was that he felt boxed in and confined, and his desire was to be free. Free to do whatever he wanted, whenever he wanted.

One day, after 9 years of employment at UPS, he called it quits. It wasn't a rash decision, but a calculated one. A year prior to working at UPS, he saw the opportunity to build a business selling birds, 9 years later, he had a $50,000 a year business selling birds and no longer needed to work his job at UPS. Today he still sells his birds all over California and has branched out to many other businesses, real estate rental properties, book writing, buying and selling cars, etc.

Sam is a dyed-in-the-wool entrepreneur. No matter what life throws at Sam, he will find a way around it, over it, under it, or even through it. Being able to adapt and change to his situation in life, he will never work a job again. Even if his bird business fails, his rental properties burn down, and his investments are destroyed, he will find a way to make money without a job.

What it Takes to Quit Your Job

So, what does it take to be able to live a life never working a job again? What separates people like Sam from everyone else? Those who are relegated to work day in and day out for someone else waiting for retirement? The answer is easier than it might seem. It is not a rich inheritance, winning the lottery, or marrying into money (although those can really help), No.

The answer is one word:

Drive

Those who have already quit their job, like Sam, have the drive to push themselves to new heights, new limits, and new destinations. Without having his drive, Sam would have given up many times when his business was struggling.

AN ENTREPRENEUR IS SOMEONE WHO TAKES RISKS, GOES OUT ON THEIR OWN, AND PUSHES THROUGH EVERYTHING THAT STANDS IN THE WAY OF THEM BEING WHO THEY WANT TO BE AND DOING WHAT THEY WANT TO DO.

Sam could have given up with any one of these setbacks:

1. A bird virus almost wiped out his entire inventory of birds
2. The government passed a law that no animals could be sold at swap-meets
3. His largest customer, PetSmart, left him for a competitor
4. His supplier did not have the inventory he needed to satisfy his customers for months

Even though these huge problems could have stopped Sam, he continued pushing, continued growing, and continued his businesses.

The business application of having drive can be summed up quite succinctly:

Entrepreneurship

An entrepreneur is someone who takes risks, goes out on their own, and pushes through everything that stands in their way of being who they want to be and doing what they want to do. They start companies, build businesses, and create money from nothing.

Being an entrepreneur, your business begins and ends with you. There is no boss, shareholder, or person dictating to you what you can or cannot do. You are the boss. You are in control. Ultimately, you are responsible if the business is a success or failure. Real entrepreneurs push through all things that get in their way and make their business successful.

Your businesses will have both good and bad times. What will set you apart from others who never make it is your ability to keep going. No matter what may get in the way of your success. That is how you will be able to quit your job and live the life you want.

Be determined to succeed.

"The best time to plant a tree was 20 years ago. The second-best time is now." - Chinese Proverb

---

The Second Best Time

He hung his head as he contemplated what we just discussed.

Rick, a co-worker of mine wanted to discuss how I got all my rental properties and was building my business.

"You are years ahead of me and I am in no place to do what you are doing. I have bills, children, my job," Rick said to me with a sad tone in his voice.

"You don't think I have those too?" I asked.

"Of course you do, but yours are 5 years ahead of me," he said.

"You need to realize I started right where you are now, the only difference is that forced myself to start, even when I didn't feel ready," I continued. "If you don't get started now, what makes you think you will start a year, two years, or three years from now? Unless you make the change now, you will still be in the same place you are now, just three years older."

As I tried to help my friend understand the possibilities of passive income, rental properties, businesses and freedom without a job, he couldn't see the forest through the trees. He was focused on the problems at hand and couldn't get out of being reactionary. What he needed was to become proactive, not reactive to the situations in his life.

It took me 9 years to build my businesses up enough to replace my income from my job. This 9 years is not a magical time-line or formula but is how long it took me to quit my job. Going from no business to a business that you can live on will most likely not come overnight. There is no get-rich-quick scheme that will help you get there. Just hard work, perseverance, and dedication to your goal.

Whatever is holding you back from starting down the path to quit your job, don't let that stop you anymore. No matter where you are in your life, make a commitment to yourself. Commit to pursuing a life without a job by building passive income and businesses that will help you become free.

To be successful in business, you don't need to be creative. You don't need to be wealthy. You don't even need a college education. What you do need to do, is to become an entrepreneur.

TAKE ACTION

What obstacles are holding you back from starting, growing, or developing your entrepreneurial business right now? List them here:

1. ______________________________

2. ______________________________

3. ______________________________

Like Sam, how can you overcome these obstacles with the "Drive" of an entrepreneur and be successful? Brainstorm below:

____

____

____

____

To become an entrepreneur, you need to think like one. Imagine all your obstacles as problems to be solved. Tackle these obstacles KNOWING that you will be successful. Write below what your life will be like once you have overcome these obstacles and are successfully unemployed.

____

____

____

____

Now, visualize yourself victorious over these obstacles and apply your "Drive" to blast through them.

CHAPTER SEVEN

LESSON 4

WORKING ON OR IN YOUR BUSINESS

"The critical ingredient is getting off your butt and doing something. It's as simple as that. A lot of people have ideas, but there are few who decide to do something about them now. Not tomorrow. Not next week. But today. The true entrepreneur is a doer, not a dreamer."

– Nolan Bushnell

The grin on his face was ear to ear.

Shaking hands as people walked in the door, laughing with a retired Army veteran, conversing with the local elderly ladies who had breakfast at 10am every Wednesday, hustling back and forth between all his guests. He was in his element. Tony, a retired dish washer is now the owner of two local breakfast houses where he could be found greeting all his guests who were dining in his restaurant.

"Hey Tony, how many hours did you work today?" I asked him one day.

"Three hours. Woke up at 8:00am, had breakfast with my amazing wife, hung out with the kids, got into the restaurant around 9:30am, then left around 1:30pm and went home and took a nap. Oh, and I had lunch with some friends in the middle there for an hour. So, technically 2 hours," he replied with a childish grin.

We were sitting in his favorite booth. This is the perfect spot in the corner of the restaurant where he can see everything going on from this one location. Like a catcher on a baseball field, from this one position, Tony could see everything going on in the entire place. With his back to the wall, he could see if something is amiss, and would be on top of it.

"Amazing, is this every day for you?" I asked.

"Oh no, that is not usual. I usually work only one hour," he said jokingly. This is why I have affectionately named him Chief Crazy Talk. He loves to laugh and have a good time. But, when it comes to his business and getting work done, he is a hard worker.

"Seriously though," he continued. "I don't work anymore than I have to, I work hard at not working hard."

"What do you mean by that?" I asked.

"I don't want to work <u>IN</u> my business. That is why I have a general manager, assistant managers, senior servers, cooks, bussers, and other employees who work <u>IN</u> the business. I spend my time the way I want to spend it," he replied.

"Wouldn't you make more money if you didn't have a general manager and did her job?" I asked.

"Sure, I would. I would make a lot more money. I pay her very well. I pay all my assistant managers well. But then I would have to do her job and I don't want to. My time is better spent building the business, finding new customers, figuring out marketing, planning for the future, etc... My time is more valuable when I work ON the business not IN the business," Tony said as our lunch arrived.

We began to eat some catfish and chips as I asked him to explain a bit more on his philosophy of not working IN your business but instead, working ON your business.

"Think about it. Washing dishes is a fine thing to do and it is a job that needs to be done, but I can pay someone else to do it. Same thing goes with serving, bussing tables, or even managing the store. I can pay someone else to do that too. What I can't do is pay someone to see the things I see or grow the business like I want it to be grown. Also, building the business is what I like to do. I don't mind washing dishes at all, but I only have so much time to give to my business and it is best spent building the business," he explained.

"Two hours a day..." I said jokingly.

"Exactly," Chief Crazy Talk said with a grin.

"I only work when I want to and do what I want to do. If I don't want to do it, I pay someone else to do it," he said.

"What if you don't have the money to pay someone else to do the work because the business is lacking in sales, income, or some other way to pay your employees?" I asked.

"If I can't afford to hire someone for a job that needs to get done, I find a way to make enough money to pay that person. If I can't afford a dish washer right now, all I need to do is focus my time on increasing my total sales by $20 per hour. I hire employees for one of two reasons: To make me money or to make my life easier, that is it. If they don't fulfill one of these functions, they are a waste of money to me. If I work ON my business and increase sales by $20 an hour, that pays for all the expenses of my new dishwasher I will hire," he said.

"So, you focus all your time and effort to work ON your business rather than IN it. Focusing on building the business rather than washing dishes," I said. Tony nodded in agreement and smiled.

As we were finishing up our lunch at his bustling restaurant, he said one final thing to me. "It is hard work to not have to work hard. It is something that you must put effort into. It doesn't come easy. Those who must control everything and everyone in their lives will not make it far in business. You need to let others take the load off your shoulders so you can build your business by working ON your business, not IN it."

Your Business Needs You In Order To Grow

Being a business owner while having a job, you may be asking yourself, "Should I hire someone to do the work for me?" This question is one every business owner must ask themselves. In reality, the answer depends on if you want to be working ON your business or IN your business AND if you want to grow your business or not.

BEING AN ENTREPRENEUR IS ALL ABOUT GETTING PAID FOR THE VALUE THAT YOU BRING, NOT THE HOURS THAT YOU WORK.

Depending what type of business you are starting, it may be wise to hire out certain aspects to others. For instance, a real estate rental business would be an easy business to hire people, especially when the properties are in another state. If you managed your rental properties yourself, you would make more money on each property per month, because you are saving the money you would normally pay to a Property Manager. The issue is you are spending your time working IN your business rather than ON it.

The key to building a business is to not actually do the work yourself, but pay someone else to do the work for you. The entrepreneurial way is to build the business in a way that it is automated to run without you. When you hire employees, even though you are not working on your business, it is still working for you making you money.

Your responsibility, as a business owner, is to work ON the business, not IN the business. The difference between those two words is dramatic in its effect on your life. The reason why I got into investing in real estate was to not have a job but be personally independent. I got tired and fed up with doing tasks needed to make the organization run.

If I worked an hour, I got paid an hourly wage for that hour. Instead, I wanted to get paid for the value that I bring, not the hours that I put in. Being an Entrepreneur allows me to do just that.

Working "IN" Your Business

Many of us have had numerous jobs in our lives. Be it hourly, salary, or commission based jobs, it doesn't matter how you get paid. You are getting paid for the hours that you put in or the work that you do. If you do not go to work, service your customers or do the job, you do not get paid. Your job is completely dependent on you doing the work.

Being an Entrepreneur is all about getting paid for the value that you bring, not the hours that you work. When you build a business, you have the opportunity to make your income truly passive by developing a strong business with a great team. The reason why your income is passive is that you still make money if you do nothing. The team members that you put on your team are the ones that work IN your business to make you money.

With a business, you are no longer an employee. Gone are the days when you clock in to work, get your two mandatory 15 minute breaks, your 30-minute lunch, and then clock out and go home. That is what employees do. You are now the employer. It is now your responsibility to make sure that your employees are the ones that make the business run. Your goal should be to do as little as possible and make the most money from other people's efforts. There is a quote from John D. Rockefeller that sums this up very well.

"I would rather earn 1% off 100 people's efforts than 100% off my own efforts."

- John D. Rockefeller

In my real estate rental property business where I am already investing, I usually spend about three hours in total buying a property, fixing it up, and renting it out. Honestly, only three hours in total. In my business, I am responsible for finding, evaluating, and purchasing an investment property. After that, I let my team do what they do best, which is get the property rented.

All but one of my many properties I purchased without stepping foot into the property. I have not even seen it in person, but only through pictures, inspection reports, and quotes for repairs from contractors, etc. What I need is specific information from them to help me know which property to buy. That information can come from any source that I trust and I make a decision to proceed or not, based on the information.

I invest in locations that are thousands of miles away from me and it would be impractical for me to physically view each one. That is why I trust my team to give me the right information when selecting a property for purchase. I do not work <u>IN</u> my business but work <u>ON</u> my business.

Working "On" Your Business

So, what are your personal responsibilities within your business? If you set up your business right, you will do all your work up front when you purchase the property, but little to nothing after that. The majority of my work is done when I set up the company.

Here are some key areas that I work ON my business:

Find a Location

I personally like to invest out of my area, far away from where I live. The reason why is because I find a greater return for my money invested in areas outside of California. For example, I bought and rehabbed a property for $23,000 and currently get $650 per month in rent from it.

Personally Visit the Area

Since I invest all over the country, I fly into the area to make sure this it's a place I want to invest in. The goal for the trip is to: meet/interview potential team members and drive the location to get a sense of the area and if it is a place I would like to invest in. I also look at any properties that are currently listed for sale. This is not necessarily to buy one I look at, but is more so that I can see the quality and type of construction in the area.

Assemble my Team

After I get back from the area, I contact the team members I want to work with and place them on my team. I always keep a list of other team members I interviewed and did not select in case I need them in the future.

Acquire a Property

The first property you buy in an area is always the most time consuming because you are still developing your business and do not have all the pieces in place yet. You need to get the contractors, the Property Manager, Realtor, inspectors, etc. in place so they can do their part.

Put my Team to Work Getting the Property Rented

After you know how each of your team members work, you are able to work more efficiently and acquire properties much faster because you know how to best utilize each team member.

Working ON your business is to do all the things that make your business grow. Fixing a plumbing leak in one of your rental properties is NOT working ON your business. That is something that you can pay an hourly employee to do.

If you pay a handyman $75 to fix a plumbing leak that you can do yourself, you have saved yourself 2.5 hours to do anything else. It is your responsibility as the business owner to use your time in a way to make your business grow. You could spend your time finding another property that will make you even more money than the $75 you paid a plumber.

For example, if it takes me two and half hours to fix a plumbing leak, I would save approximately $75 for my time. Right now, it may seem like saving $75 for two hours and a half of your life would be good if you are currently making $15 an hour. Your hourly rate would actually be $30 an hour since you are making $75 by spending two and a half hours of your life like you would in a normal job. $75 divided by 2.5 equals $30 an hour. But, what about the opportunity cost of that two and a half hours?

Opportunity Cost: The cost of an alternative that must be forgone in order to pursue a certain action.

If you spent two and half hours buying another rental property that may make you $3,600 in one year, then the $75 you saved doing your own plumbing could cost you $3,600 because you missed out on a property.

Working ON your business instead of spending the two and half hours buying one rental property will bring you almost an unlimited hourly rate. Think about it. You buy a rental property that takes you almost five hours to purchase.

If you got paid a specific dollar amount for the work you put in, that would be your hourly wage. What is fantastic about passive income investing in real estate is that you continually get paid for the same five hours of work you put in until you sell the property. Only after you sell the property would you be able to calculate your hourly wage because your pay goes on and on.

Here is a quick example of how long it takes me to acquire a new property for rent:

- Step 1. Locate and identify the potential investment property
  - 0 hours.
  - I have realtors working all the time finding me properties to evaluate and possibly purchase. They get paid when I buy a property, so it is up to them to work hard to find me a property to buy.
- Step 2. Evaluate the list of potential properties
  - 1 to 2 hours.
  - I have the contractor and property manager go through the property to find all the issues with the property and estimate repair costs. After I have assessed the total cost to rehab the property, I deduct the total from the asking price.
- Step 3. Analyze the numbers
  - 1 hour.
  - This step is important to make sure that the property is worth pursuing. I want to check the cash flow of the property to make sure it is a good investment.
- Step 4. Have my realtor present the offer to the seller
  - 0 hours.

  - This step does not take any time at all because the realtor does all the work.
- Step 5. Sign the contract
  - 10 min.
  - The realtor emails me the contract which will save a lot of time, print out the contract, sign on the appropriate locations in the contract and send the scanned image of the contract back.
- Step 6. Open escrow
  - 0 hours.
  - No time taken because the realtor and title company do all the work.
- 7. Property inspections
  - 10 minutes
  - My property manager will schedule all the inspections I feel are necessary. The inspectors then send me the report via email when they are finished. Reviewing the inspections go very quick. With experience, it will be quick and easy to spot potential problems with the property.
- Step 8. Close escrow
  - 30 minutes
  - I work with the title company to transfer the funds needed for the purchase of the property. Depending on their processes and procedures, it could be as little as 10 minutes to 30 minutes to close escrow and deliver the funds, all is done electronically.
- Step 9. Rehab the property
  - 10 minutes

  - Since I have already evaluated the property and have a general idea of the work needed to be done, my property manager will manage the rehab of the property.
  - Review the before and after pictures sent by the contractors and property manager.
- Step 10. Find a tenant and sign the lease
  - 0 hours
  - Once the property is all completed, it is on my property manager to find a good tenant and sign the lease.

<u>Total: 3.6 hours</u>

So, the amount of time it would take to purchase a rental property would be about 3 ½ hours. That is only one more hour than the plumbing project that would make you $30 an hour. If this one property, that you spent 3.5 hours buying, makes you $300 a month for 12 months, you make $3,600 in the first year for your 3.5 hours of work or $1,029 per hour!

EMPLOYING OTHERS TO WORK FOR YOU WILL ALLOW YOU TO SPEND YOUR PRECIOUS TIME ON THINGS THAT ACTUALLY MAKE YOU MONEY.

Imagine if you own the property for 10 years. Just from the cash flow alone, you would earn $36,000 for your 3.5 hours of work. That is $10,285 per hour!

Employing others to work for you will allow you to spend your precious time on things that actually make you money. Or, even spend your precious time with your family instead of fixing a plumbing leak. Personally, I am glad that I invest in rental properties and use a property manager. By employing him to do all the work, I have so much more time to do the things that matter most.

I completely understand that when you are starting out investing in real estate, every penny counts and it's hard to pay out money when you don't have enough of it. If this is the case for you and you need to do the repairs yourself, your goal should be to build up your business income enough to pay someone else to do the work.

You need to work hard for a while so that you do not have to work hard in the future. What I mean is put your time into building your business now so you can employ other people to do the work for you. Your time will then be used to concentrate on the things that matter most. From now on, focus on working ON your business, not IN it.

TAKE ACTION

Name three ways you are working ***IN*** your business that you should stop right away. List them here:

1. ______________________________

2. ______________________________

3. ______________________________

Who can you give up some of your responsibilities to in your business to free you up to focus on building your business? List them below and what they should take over for you:

1. ______________________________

   ____

2. ______________________________

   ____

3. ______________________________

   ____

How can you build up your team more to allow you to work ***ON*** your business rather than ***IN*** it? List them in order here:

____

____

____

____

____

____

SECTION 2

I is for an Independent Attitude

"The important thing is not being afraid to take a chance. Remember, the greatest failure is to not try. Once you find something you love to do, be the best at doing it."

– Debbi Fields

Thinking outside of the box is what entrepreneurs do. This section about independent attitude is where you will learn to focus on how to think proactively as well as outside the box about problems that will come when you quit your job.

Every employer attracts and retains employees by paying them an hourly wage. If you think about it, every company you could ever work for wants to pay you the least amount of money they can, while keeping you working for them. If the company you work for paid you any less than you are making now, you would quit. If they paid you any more, the company would be wasting money. And companies never want to waste money.

This type of logic applies to your benefits (insurance, vacation leave, 401k matching, etc.) as an employee as well. Just because we are all taught that we need a job for the "benefits", doesn't mean that we should actually keep with that teaching. Things like health insurance, 401k, dental insurance, Social Security payments, are all items that can be accomplished without a job. Likewise, thinking independently and having an attitude that you can make it on your own, will help you answer all the problems that will arise as you quit your job.

In this section, I will answer some key reasons why some people will never quit their job. Think of these and other problems as problems that you, as an entrepreneur, must find the answer to. Necessity is the mother of invention and it is necessary that you consider these and many other potential issues that may arise. Health insurance, retirement, vacation and sick time, and other benefits are all questions you will have to answer for yourself. I have already answered them for myself and share with you my thinking as a means to get you started.

For section 2, **I stands for Independent Attitude**. This section is to help you to have an independent attitude so you can answer all these questions and more on your own. Remember, the key to being successfully unemployed is having your independence. Not being dependent on someone for a job.

CHAPTER EIGHT

LESSON 5
FINDING THE RIGHT TIME TO QUIT YOUR JOB

"Successful people are the ones who are breaking the rules."
– Seth Godin

The murky brown water drained quickly from the 75-gallon reservoir into the city sewer system. Jarod, the owner of a local carpet cleaning company, just got done cleaning his last carpet for the day. Five homes in one day is a normal occurrence for him as he continues to build his rapidly growing carpet cleaning business. Service, quality and price are the three foundations of the business he has built. The problem he solves for his customers is cleaning their dirty carpet.

As a business owner, Jarod decided long ago that he would never work a job again. Prior to owning a carpet cleaning business, Jarod was in the business of flipping houses for profit. He would find a property, buy it, remodel the inside and out and then sell it for more money than he put into it. This was his way of life before the real estate bubble burst in 2009.

Before the bubble burst, Jarod was selling houses days after he listed them for sale. After, homes were taking months to sell and only after reducing the price many times in order to get buyers interested. His business was in trouble. Prices of homes were so low that he could not find a house to buy cheap enough for him to make any money. If Jarod wasn't an entrepreneur and committed to never working for someone again, he would have gotten a job.

Instead, Jarod found a way to solve his problem by providing a service for others that solves theirs. He noticed that the tile in his kitchen was dirty and needed cleaning. He got a quote from a carpet company to clean the tile and was amazed at how expensive the quote was. Since money was tight, he looked up on the internet how to clean it himself. That is when he got the idea for his new business.

He had never cleaned carpets before, but he knew that he could figure it out. After working hard to come up with the money, he bought a $1000 carpet cleaning system that he used out of his beat-up truck. Job after job, he worked hard to save enough money to buy a carpet cleaning van with a 75-gallon carpet cleaning system contained within.

Now, years later, Jarod is still working hard at building his business while never having to get a job again. He normally charges $99 for 3 rooms and a hallway as a special. In one day, he can do 4-6 homes which would even add more rooms and areas to increase his price. That would be $400-$600 a day before his expenses and that does not even account for his ability to up-sell his services.

Even without a proven business, Jarod never took a job to earn his income. Being an entrepreneur, he found a problem and figured out a way to solve it.

Quit When Your Job Is Costing You Money

If you're like Jarod and never began working a job and immediately became an entrepreneur, or like me working years before you quit, finding the right time to go it alone and solely rely on yourself as an entrepreneur is a tricky thing. But, what it all comes down to is the level of risk you are willing to expose yourself to and how quickly you can think like an entrepreneur and solve the problem of not having income to support you and your family.

Your situation will be totally different than everyone else because your life is different and your level of risk is different. I knew that the time had come to quit my job when it was costing me money to work for someone else rather than myself. Even though I was earning $5000 a month from my job, I knew that once I quit my job I would have the ability to make much more money.

PASSIVE INCOME IS A SHIFT FROM GETTING PAID HOURLY TO GETTING PAID CONTINUOUSLY.

The types of businesses I create are based on the principle of passive income. This type of income is money that comes in whether I work or not. In contrast, Jarod's carpet cleaning business is active income. He goes to someone's house and cleans their carpet and he gets paid. If he takes a day off and does not clean anyone's carpet, there's no income generated. His rental properties on the other hand, continually pay him whether he works or not.

The term passive income has been thrown around a lot recently. People use it for things like multi-level marketing, starting a sole-proprietor business, and investing in the appreciation of stocks. The problem with these is that they are not passive. For something to be considered truly passive income, it has to fit the definition of both passive and income. Passive income is a shift from getting paid hourly to getting paid continuously.

Passive: Used to describe someone who allows things to happen or who accepts what other people do or decide without trying to change anything.

Income: Money that is earned from work, investments, business, etc.

When you put these two together, you have someone who makes money without doing anything to earn it. The only work you do is when you start the passive income business. After that, the money comes in whether you work not. I wrote extensively about this in my second book "How to Quit Your Job with Passive Income - The Ultimate Beginners Guide to Wealth and Riches with 12 Proven Businesses You Can Start Today." In it, I show how you can work one time and continually be paid month after month.

Take the time to consider your situation and your ability to tolerate risk to see if it is the right time to quit your job. For me, it was when I had enough passive income and cash flow each month to cover all expenses from my businesses. I personally did not have enough risk tolerance to quit my job sooner than that. Likewise, Sam waited until he built up his business to an income of $50,000 per year. Jarod had never actually had a job, but started working for himself after he left college.

Opportunity Cost

Your time is the most valuable thing you can spend.

What you need to consider is by continuing to work a job, what are you giving up in order to keep that job? This is called the opportunity cost. It is the loss of potential gain from other alternatives when one alternative is chosen. By working a 40-hour job, you are giving your employer 40 hours of your life that you could use doing something else that makes you even more money.

Think of it this way. If you have a job where you work 40 hours a week earning $25 an hour, you may be passing up another job where you can make $30 an hour.

$25 an hour - $30 an hour = -$5 an hour in opportunity cost

By continuing to work the $25 an hour job and not working the $30 an hour job, the opportunity cost you are losing is $5 an hour.

The opportunity cost of your time can vary depending on what other opportunities are out there. For my situation, spending 40 hours a week on my businesses would make me much more money than my job could ever pay me. Just like how my three books earned me $1500 passively in one month, if I write 40 hours a week and put out many more books for sale, my income will increase dramatically.

Don't forget that passive income is work done one time while getting paid continuously. When I write a book, create an online course, buy rental property, or build any of my passive income businesses, I do it one time and continuously receive monthly income without doing any more work. This is why working for yourself while building passive income is the most lucrative way you can spend your time.

If you were to ask me when I think it would be a good time to quit your job, I would give you two criteria:

1. When the income from your businesses exceeds your expenses each month.
2. When working your job is costing you money in the form of a loss in opportunity cost.

Quitting your job is nerve-racking enough to do it without being prepared. Making sure you have enough income that exceeds your expenses should be at the top of the list.

Find the right time, event, or situation to quit

"When is it Dustin, when is the big day?" Joe, a Lieutenant for the local Sheriff asked me with a wide grin on his face.

"To tell you the truth, it is not a specific day," I replied.

"What? Why not?" He asked.

I had to think about it for a minute. This question had been asked of me many times by many different people, but this time I really stopped to consider it. Why hadn't I picked a specific day? Even though I had been planning this for a long time now, I did not have a specific date in mind. I didn't want to give Joe a nebulous answer, so I thought hard about it and replied.

"When most people are retiring from their job, it is because they put in a certain amount of days and years into their job and have built up their retirement enough that they could quit. Their lives have been spent building up their retirement and they know it is time to quit their job because they put in enough time to get their retirement... my situation is different," I replied.

"So, if other people are waiting for a certain time requirement to quit their job and retire, what are you waiting for?" Joe asked as he began to understand my hesitation for a date.

"I am waiting for an event, not a specific date," I said.

"An event? What event will that be?" He asked.

"I am waiting for the refinance of four of my rental properties to finish before I quit my job. Banks don't take too kindly to people who quit their jobs in the middle of getting a loan from them. They only care that you will be able to repay the loan. If my income drastically drops in the middle of the loan, they would stop the process and not give me the loan I need to continue building my business," I explained.

As the conversation continued with Joe, I realized that there are many ways to pick the right time to quit your job. Eight months prior, I had already built up my business enough to quit my job but delayed quitting until the refinance actually went through.

This is a valid and useful way to choose the day to quit your job. It can be a specific date, or a situation or event that can mark the perfect time to strike out on your own. Let's say for instance that I wanted to move to Arizona from California and I was waiting to find a home there to live in before I quit my job. But, in order to buy a home, banks need you to prove you can pay back that loan. This can be a dilemma.

To top this off, I also needed to sell my current home before moving in order to save on expenses and make it more feasible for my family to survive without my job. But, I couldn't sell too early or else we wouldn't have a place to live. This is a tricky situation.

> AGAIN, THINKING LIKE ANY ENTREPRENEUR, THIS IS A PROBLEM THAT CAN BE SOLVED. IT JUST TAKES CREATIVITY AND PERSISTENCE TO SOLVE THE PROBLEM WELL.

Again, thinking like an entrepreneur, this is a problem that can be solved. It just takes creativity and persistence to solve the problem well. This was a real-life scenario for me and my wife before we moved to Arizona. There was a problem and I solved it before I quit my job.

So, planning the day to quit your job can be more than just a randomly chosen date. It can be an event, situation, or a problem to be solved in order for you to quit successfully.

Another big reason why I did not quit my job sooner was because of the 500 hours of vacation time I had saved up over the years. Working for the local county government, I earned 11.15 hours of vacation and sick time every two weeks. That time quickly accumulated to a massive amount of time to take off before I quit my job.

TAKE ACTION

When do you feel is the right time to quit your job? What date, situation, or event needs to occur before you quit?

____

____

____

____

____

What could you do to speed up the time it takes you to quit your job?

____

____

____

Make a pledge to yourself. Write the date, situation, or event that needs to occur before you quit your job. Make this a deadline for you to quit. By righting it down, you will be making a commitment to yourself to work as hard as you can to make your dream a reality.

I make the commitment to quit my job when:

____

____

____

____

Signature Date

CHAPTER NINE

LESSON 6

YOUR BOSS FOUND OUT YOU ARE QUITTING!

"All paid jobs absorb and degrade the mind."

– Aristotle

Hanging up the phone, the sense of nervousness crept all over me.

I had been planning and preparing for this day for years and now it was finally here. What would I say? How would I react? What would be his response? Would he fire me on the spot? As I walked to my boss's office, I recounted how the conversation on the phone went:

"This is Dustin," I said as I answered my work phone.

"Dustin, could you come to my office?" My boss asked.

"Sure," I replied.

As I hung up the phone, I had a funny feeling this was going to be

TALKING ABOUT YOUR BUSINESS IS SOMETHING THAT YOU MUST DO IF YOU ARE GOING TO GET AHEAD, BUT THE MORE PEOPLE YOU TALK TO, THE SOONER YOUR BOSS MAY HEAR ABOUT IT.

the conversation that I knew would eventually come. Nothing was said that lead me to feel that way, but I just knew today was the day. The biggest question on my mind was, "How did he find out?" It couldn't have been my blog (insert sarcasm) that shared with the world that I was going to quit my job in 2017.

Just about everyone wants to say "I QUIT" to their boss at some point in their life. But what do you do if your boss asks you if you are going to quit and retire early? Successful business owners realize that it takes a team of people to run a strong and profitable business. You should not solely rely on yourself to run and build your business. You never know when the next deal or idea might come from someone you would never have expected. But, in doing that, word will get out quickly that you plan to quit.

Talking about your business is something that you must do if you are going to get ahead, but the more people you talk to, the sooner your boss may hear about it. And if you are planning to quit, you must expect that word will get back to your boss.

If you are creating a real estate investing business, creating a blog or podcast, or even writing a book, you need other people on your team if you want your business to grow quickly. When you invest in rental properties, talking about your business just becomes a part of your natural language. Conversations tend to lead back to you and your business. People will begin to ask how your business is doing, your plan for the future, and how you can quit early, etc.

Since most people retire around the ripe old age of 68, your plan to retire at the age of 35 will come as a shock to most. Your co-workers may have a variety of different reactions when they find out about your plans. Some may be very happy for you, while others may be envious and look to harm your future with your employer. In either case, you need to prepare in advance for what's going to happen when others find out about your plan.

"I QUIT"

It was no secret that I had been investing in real estate for over 8 years. In fact, when I first got hired, I was specifically asked about my investment properties. I didn't hide anything and never desired to. I put down on my resume that I own a business that invests in rental properties. I even included my previous retail business that I started, owned for four years and then successfully sold.

My employer knew that I had many businesses and projects outside of my job before they hired me and they were fine with it. Even though they knew, I never directly told them my plan to quit. I figured, why rock the boat? There was no need to tell them my plan, so I kept it to myself. With my blog, though, many people would be able to see my plan, so I was prepared for the inevitable conversation with my boss.

"I heard a rumor that you were planning on quitting soon."

My boss wasted no time in asking me as straight forward as possible.

"Yep, sure am," I replied without hesitation.

Taken a little aback by my direct answer, he asked, "Oh, well, how soon?"

"I don't have a specific date at the moment. There are a few things I need to do in my businesses before I can do that," I said.

"Okay, could you tell me about your plan? What are you going to do after you quit?" He inquired.

As I began to explain my thought process, 10-year plan, current business strategy, etc., I could see that my boss was very intrigued.

Intrigued, if not actually desirous of the position that I had put myself in. The conversation went on for 5 minutes or so and ended with me walking out of the office with my head held high. I felt like a million bucks.

What was my boss going to do? Fire me because I was planning to quit? Maybe. But, no one ever gets fired working for the government. There are too many rules, regulations, CYA, lawyers, unions, etc. There was no way he was going to fire me. Also, there was nothing he could hang over my head. I didn't need the job anymore, so he couldn't really threaten me. I was elated.

My situation is different from that of most people. If you work in the private sector, your employer may just fire you. Most states are "At Will" employment. This means an employer can hire or fire for any or no reason (as long as it's not discrimination). But if you are a good employee, hopefully your boss will want to keep you around for as long as possible.

So, how are you going to handle the awkward conversation when your boss asks you, "I heard a rumor that you are going to quit soon?"

Think of these things beforehand so you will be ready for the conversation.

Decide What You Are Going to Say In Advance

Before you get to that conversation with your boss, know what you're going to say. The last thing you want to do is go into this conversation making things up. It may not be necessary to role-play with someone before you meet with your boss, but be ready to respond how you feel best fits your situation.

I knew beforehand my answer to the question, "Are you quitting sometime in the near future?"

Since I had already put my plan on my blog, it was easy to be open and honest. Your situation may be different though. Your boss and coworkers may not have any clue what you're doing or how well you're doing. I was straightforward and honest about my business and told the truth about everything. I personally believe there is no reason to lie, even if my boss might try to fire me.

Analyze Your Current Employment

There are two things you need to look at when you analyze your employment.

Your job and your boss. Each job is different and each boss will have a different reaction to your plan to quit your job. Let's start with what type of job you have and what company you work for.

Public-Sector

There are generally two different types of jobs you can have: private sector and public-sector. If you work in the public-sector, local, state, and federal government jobs, then you should not have anything to worry about. It is as if the public-sector jobs are a protected class. The government does not like to fire people because they do not want to get sued.

I worked in the public-sector for over 14 years and have seen many people who should be fired for incompetence, inability to perform, or even insubordination. Rather than being fired, they continue to work year after year until they retire in their 60's.

Some would even sleep at their desk, purposely, and not be fired. There are many employees in the public-sector that I would never hire for any of my businesses. Even more so, they would never keep a job in the private sector because they would be fired. I will say, however, that there are many good employees that work in the public-sector, but these are far and few between.

Private-Sector

If you work in the private-sector, it is much easier for your employer to fire you. Depending on what state you live in, it may be easy for an employer to fire an employee. In California for example, the state is an "at will" employment state. So, if you work in a private sector company that does not have a union, you are at risk of your employer finding some way to fire you to get someone that will be more of a long-term employee.

IF YOUR BOSS IS THE TYPE THAT TAKES ALL THE CREDIT AND PLACES ALL THE BLAME, THEN IT MAY BE WISE TO BE CONCERNED ABOUT RETALIATION.

Your Boss

The other factor you need to think about is who your boss is.

Is your boss the type that is easy-going and wants what's best for you, or is your boss someone who only looks out for his/herself? Does your boss take all the credit for the good work you do? Does he blame others when he screws up?

If your boss is the type that takes all the credit and places all the blame, then it may be wise to be concerned about retaliation. You may have a boss who is insecure and selfish, who will fire you when he finds out that you plan to quit. Jealousy will consume him/her and he will want to get rid of you out of spite. Conversely, if your boss is a leader who gives all the credit and takes all the blame, you may be in good hands. If your boss desires the best for you, he may take it well and be encouraged by you.

In either case, use your judgment of your boss's character before you go into the conversation.

The Human Resources Department

The human resources department of your job is there to help you and will do everything they can to make sure that you keep your job. If, for some reason, your boss wants to fire you because you plan to quit in a year, you have to keep your boss playing by the rules.

The HR department tries to keep the company from getting sued so they are always watching to protect from any miss-steps of their employees. The HR department is there to protect your rights from your employer as well as protect the company. They should keep everything that you say confidential and not tell your boss. Even though that's the case, you need to be very selective of whom you trust with your secrets.

Just remember that they are not your friends. They work for the employer too and they want to keep their job. Their job is to keep the company out of lawsuits with its employees. Get information out of them but don't consider them on your side. I suggest asking questions that hint around your plan without divulging your plan to HR representative. When you talk with them, you don't have to be specific.

You could ask questions like:

1. As I plan for my retirement in the future, should I worry about my boss being upset that I am going to retire and fire me?"
2. "If my boss is trying to fire me for an unfounded reason, what recourse do I have?"
3. "How am I protected from unlawful termination?"

As always, your situation is different from everyone else and so you have to figure out the best strategy for your situation. A great head start would be for you to grab the employee manual for your company to read for yourself the policies that are in place for your job. You may get all your questions answered by reading the policy without having anybody get suspicious.

Honesty Is the Best Policy

When it comes time for that awkward conversation with your boss, honesty is the best policy. Lying about you quitting your job will not make anything better and it might even make things worse. If you have integrity and are upfront and honest, he may be surprised that you are.

I thought about this conversation with my boss for a long time and knew what I was going to say. When he asked me about my retirement, I told him the truth. "Yes, I am absolutely planning on retiring early because my rental properties and passive income make me enough money so that I don't have to work anymore."

He asked a few more questions about my plan, but all in all, it was a fine conversation and one that was almost easy-going. Personally, I am glad that my boss found out that I was quitting early. This had the surprising benefit of reducing my workload and freeing me up to focus on my businesses. I shared with him all my investments and my plan to retire early because I really enjoy helping people understand how great passive income is and how anyone can do it.

Say As Little As Possible

You don't owe your boss an explanation for anything outside of work that you do that does not hurt the company. You also don't need to give your life story. If you feel like keeping your cards close to your chest (poker term for not showing what you have in your hand) then you don't have to. Keep the conversation loose and "matter-of-fact."

The conversation could go like this:

Boss: "So, there is a rumor that you plan to quit sometime soon."

You: "Ya"

Boss: "Can you tell me when so I don't get taken off guard?"

You: "Sure. Within a year or two. How much notice would you want me to give?"

Boss: "A couple months would be great."

You: "No problem. Bye."

It is up to you how much you want to share about your plans. It is your life and you are free to make your decisions the way you want.

Be Ready for Retaliation

What if you have a boss that is vindictive and resentful of your success? There are plenty of horrible boss's out there that only care about themselves and use people for their own benefit. If your boss is this type of human being, then you need to be ready for him to do everything he can to fire you before you have a chance to quit your job.

First thing is to keep it a secret as long as you can. Take it from me, creating a blog, writing a book, and telling people that you are going to quit your job in six months is not the best way to keep it a secret.

YOU SHOULD GET PAID FOR THE VALUE YOU BRING, NOT THE HOURS YOU PUT IN. YOUR LIFE BELONGS TO YOU AND IT SHOULD NOT REVOLVE AROUND YOUR JOB.

Even though it's hard to not talk about all the great things that are going on, do your best to keep those things only to those that are closest to you that will keep your secret. Only share with people that are outside of your normal community of friends and coworkers to build your business.

Set Your Date and Stick to It

You have no obligation to stay at your job any longer than you desire.

You may have a job where your boss believes he really needs you to keep the business running. If that were the case, then he should pay you more! No matter how much your boss wants you to stay working there for the next 20 years, you need to resist.

Personally, I would only continue working if I received two things:

1. The job on my terms. I could make my own schedule, come and go as I please, and make sure my work gets done better than if I were working there 40+ hours a week.
2. If I got paid for what I believe I am worth, not what my employer believes I am worth.

You should get paid for the value you bring, not the hours you put in. Your life belongs to you and it should not revolve around your job. Only when you are a business owner, building your own business, should your life revolve around your business.

Always Have a Backup Plan

Knowing that being fired prematurely is always a possibility, you need to have a backup plan ready to implement in case you do get fired before you quit. If you fail to plan, you plan to fail.

Without a backup plan, you may get stuck without a job as you are building your businesses. It is hard to get financing for rental properties when you do not have a W-2 job that brings in earned income.

Your personal situation is different from everyone else's, so having a backup plan can only be developed by you around your situation.

Example: My backup plan

- Build my business as fast as possible.
- Educate myself on more ways to make money in real estate outside of rental properties.
- Know how to make cash quick from buying and selling houses.

- Know what items I can sell that I do not need in my life and downsize.
- Be ready to move out of my house and move into a smaller house that costs less.
- Sell my current house to make more income to pay for the smaller house.
- Network with as many other investors as possible for potential partnerships.
- Develop other streams of passive income through blogs, podcasts, books, etc.
- Know where I have the possibility to get a job to earn some income while my business grows.

Don't Burn Bridges. Unless you really want to...

No matter what situation you find yourself in with your job, do your best to never burn any bridges. Burning a bridge is effectively making sure your employer will never hire you again. You never know what life may throw at you and it's possible you could go back to your employer and ask for your job back, if necessary.

It may be wise to have the ability to go back to your job if something unexpected happens with your passive income business. You also never know where your next deal or partner may come from. Your employer, coworkers, or customers may be a great opportunity for you and your businesses.

A Horrible Job = Burn the Bridge Down!

It could be the case where you KNOW you should never work this job again and you want to make sure of it.

Think of an army going into enemy territory. As the army goes over one bridge to engage the enemy, they burn down the bridge so there is no retreat of their own soldiers or allow the enemy to advance into their territory. The only option is to move forward and conquer the next area or die. Hence, they burned each bridge after they crossed it.

Necessity is the mother of invention,
especially in business.

If you need to make money and can't go back to your original job, then you will probably work hard at inventing other ways to make money. In your drive to build your businesses, you may just need to burn some bridges as you go to make sure that the only option is to press on and build a successful business.

It seems inevitable to me that your boss will find out that you plan to quit your job before you hit retirement age. The best advice I can give is for you to think through the conversation before you have it. When you have already thought through the conversation, you will not be caught off guard and be put on the defensive.

One other thing is; **Don't sweat it**.

Don't worry about your boss finding out. Don't let that stop you from building your passive income business to quit your job. If you let that stop you, then you have already failed. You will never know what it's like to not have to work for someone ever again.

TAKE ACTION

Take a good hard look at your current employment. How will your boss take it when he finds out? Will you need to talk with the Human Relations department? (if there is one) Can you be fired on the spot? Write your answers below.

____

____

____

____

Think about your backup plan. What can you do to make sure that you will be fine if your boss fires you on the spot? Write your backup plan below:

1. ____
2. ____
3. ____
4. ____
5. ____
6. ____

Plan out right now what you are going to say to your boss when he finds out you are planning on quitting your job. Try to make it short and to the point.

____

____

____

____

____

CHAPTER TEN

LESSON 7

What to Do With Your Vacation and Sick Time

"So often people are working hard at the wrong thing. Working on the right thing is probably more important than working hard."

– Caterina Fake

Melissa couldn't contain her excitement.

Just 3 hours into the flight, she was already picturing herself in the historic place where Paul Revere rode yelling that the British were coming, experiencing the beautiful fall foliage, walking the freedom trail, seeing the U.S.S. Constitution, and climbing up the 294 stairs in the monument for the Battle of Bunker Hill.

It had been years since she was last on a vacation and she had looked forward to this day for months. The last time she was on a vacation without her children was 10 years prior. Looking out the window at the U.S., she couldn't believe she was actually on her way to a 2-week vacation without the kids. Here is her story:

10 years ago, we were married and took our Honeymoon to Jamaica at an all-inclusive resort on the coastal town of Negril. The crystal clear blue waters, the fantastic food, the entertainment, and the relaxation of being on an island away from everything made us feel tremendously blessed. Being our one and only trip alone together, this was my favorite vacation we had ever taken, until now.

Four kids and a lot of hard work to quit my job and we were alone again. Flying to another place where we could enjoy each other, see amazing historical sites, see good friends, and just spend time doing what we wanted to do. This time, we were flying to Boston for our 10-year anniversary. Not many people earn enough vacation time from their work to take 2 weeks off work, let alone 4 months in one year.

480 hours.

That is how much sick leave and vacation time I had accumulated over the 13 years working for the county government. It's not like I never took time off. In fact, I was required to take at least 120 hours of leave time each year. In working for the government for so long, every two weeks, I was accruing 11.18 hours of vacation and sick leave. So, you can imagine how my bank of vacation time grew quickly.

I understand that most employees are not as blessed as I am to have such a wonderful job. Such a wonderful job in fact that in the last year that I worked, I had taken over 640 hours of vacation time from my work and spent it over the course of seven months.

Here is how I spent it:

- June 2016 – Six weeks off to remodel my master bathroom and write my second book.

- August 2016 – Two-week guys trip to Ketchikan Alaska for an amazing deer hunting and deep-sea fishing trip with two good friends.
- October 2016 – Two-week 10-year anniversary trip to Boston.
- December 2016 – Four weeks off to remodel the rest of our home and spend the rest of my vacation time.

I had the blessing of having many hours of vacation time saved up as well as the ability to earn many more as I continue to work for my job. But, what do you do with those banked vacation/sick hours that you have earned?

What if you have 300+ hours of vacation time saved up from your job? Should you cash it out when you quit or should you do something else with it? I started my plan with 480 hours of vacation time. With that, I had to plan the best strategy to use my vacation time. Remember the goal is to quit working and not need the vacation time.

So, is it better to cash out or spend your vacation time from your job?

Cashing Out Your Vacation Time All At Once?

The first option that most employees take, is really the worst of two options. Anytime you get a large lump sum of money, it feels very good. When you get a large inheritance, win the lottery, or cash out your vacation time, it can be very exhilarating. In the case of your vacation time, is cashing it out for a lump sum really a good thing?

If we penciled out the pros and cons with cashing out your vacation time there really is only one for each.

Pro: *Large sum of money paid on the day you retire.*

Con: *The large sum is heavily taxed.*

When you look at the amount that would be taken out in taxes, this one problem should dissuade you from going with the cash out option. Almost half of the money you earned will be taken by the government. A good estimate is that 40% of your lump sum will go directly to the government without even entering into your pocket.

If you're like me, you hate paying taxes and try your best to avoid or defer them as much as legally possible. I do believe, however, that we should give to Caesar what belongs to Caesar and to God what is God's. So, never cheat on your taxes, but you should do everything legally possible to avoid and/or defer them to a much later date.

After I considered the huge negative to my (albeit good) problem of having a lot of vacation time to cash out, I knew there had to be a better option.

The Better Option For Your Vacation Time

Think about what happens when you take a vacation from your job. Do you not get all the benefits of having a job while not working? Being on vacation is almost as good as not actually having a job altogether. You still get your paycheck like normal, you are still employed, and you continue to earn benefits as if you were working your normal hours at your job.

Let's stay on the idea of the benefits from your job. Most good jobs have some or all the following:

- Accrue vacation time while you work.
- Accrue retirement.
- You and your employer continue to contribute to a 401k or IRA.
- Health care is provided by your employer.
- You receive a regular paycheck every two weeks.
- You are employed.

- Taxed at your normal tax rate.
- You can use your job to get financing for cars, properties, etc.

Wouldn't it be nice to still be employed, get paid your normal salary, still get your health insurance, contribute to your retirement, and earn more vacation time, all while you have already quit working? Yes, that would be amazing. The next best thing to quitting your job is to be paid with your accumulated vacation and to still have the benefits that come with being employed.

ONE OF THE BEST THINGS ABOUT SPENDING YOUR VACATION TIME, RATHER THAN CASHING IT OUT, IS THAT YOU EARN MORE VACATION TIME!

By doing this, most jobs still allow you to earn even MORE vacation time! If you think about it, when you actually spend your vacation hours, you are still employed, you earn more vacation hours while you are actually not working. In my case, since I earn 11.18 hours every two weeks, I could take a two-week vacation, spend 80 hours for that vacation and earn 11.18 more hours during my vacation!

So, one two-week vacation actually only costed me 68.82 hours instead of the normal 80 hours. When I quit my job, I had 480 hours of vacation time banked to spend. If I spent all those 480 hours, I would earn another 67 hours.

480 hours/40 hours a week = 12 weeks vacation
12 Weeks vacation spent = 67 more hours of vacation earned

Total hours needed to spend: 480+67=**547 hours!**

With that premise in mind, think of how you can use your vacation time to your advantage. Maybe save up all your vacation hours for when you quit your job and spend them at the very end when you're ready to quit. Your situation would be different than mine and your employer will probably be different too. If you are going to spend your vacation time to get all these benefits, you need to think like an entrepreneur and solve this problem.

Solve the Vacation Time Problem

ANOTHER CREATIVE WAY TO SPEND YOUR TIME WOULD BE TO TAKE MANY MINI VACATIONS THROUGHOUT THE YEAR. 1 WEEK HERE, 2 WEEKS THERE, AND EVENTUALLY SPEND ALL YOUR TIME.

How will you get your employer's permission to spend all your vacation?

For example, let's say you're going to quit your job on June 1st and that is the day that you will stop actually working. If your boss doesn't know that you are going to quit, you could ask for a long vacation. I would recommend asking 6 to 8 months in advance for a nice long two-month vacation in order to take your family across the country on a road trip. Hopefully your boss would approve this once in a lifetime chance to spend the full summer break traveling the US with your children.

Another creative way to spend your time would be to take many mini vacations throughout the year. 1 week here, 2 weeks there, and eventually spend all your time. Maybe even a combination of both of these strategies, where you take one large vacation and three smaller ones. It is your problem to solve, and a great problem to have!

If you have the ability to spend your vacation time well, you will have mentally already quit your job while continually getting paid for your vacation hours. On top of that, you are still earning more vacation time while you're not working. Solving this one problem correctly will give you a few extra months of paychecks coming in, while not paying a huge lump sum in taxes.

Once it is time for you to spend your vacation time, get creative and think of as many ways you can spend those vacation hours without having any trouble with your boss.

TAKE ACTION

How much vacation time do you currently have?

____

How much vacation/sick time do you accrue every pay period?

____

How much time would you gain if you spent all your vacation/sick time before you quit your job?

____

When it is time to use your vacation/sick time, what trips or activities will you use to request the time off?

1. ______________________________________

2. ______________________________________

3. ______________________________________

4. ______________________________________

What problems do you anticipate your boss using to object to your vacation request? Write them below and spend some time solving these problems before your boss can make an issue of them.

____

____

____

____

CHAPTER ELEVEN

LESSON 8

WHAT TO DO ABOUT HEALTH INSURANCE

"Risk more than others think is safe. Dream more than others think is practical."

-Howard Schultz

It wasn't his fault.

Even though he was 78 years old, he was still working his job for the local county government for over 50 years. Roger, a loving husband of 60 years couldn't quit his job. His plan to retire at age 64 passed him up long ago. He had planned to spend his retirement years with his wife traveling the world doing things they always wanted to do.

At age 53, he and Debbie had the opportunity to travel to Italy to see the Sistine Chapel with some friends. Instead of going, Roger convinced himself and Debbie that this sort of trip can wait. He told her they needed to save their money for their retirement and once they were retired, they would travel the world together.

When he was 62 years old, his wife Debbie (at the age of 61) was diagnosed with a debilitating disease. She could barely get out of bed let alone get on a plane and travel to a distant country. Their plans for retirement had faded and Roger continued to work because he needed to keep his health insurance going for his wife.

Because of his love for his wife, he feels blessed that he gets to do this for her. It is not a burden for him as some may expect. He believes that love is an action that he can show his wife every day by his service to her.

Now, imagine if Roger had quit his job when he was 53 years old because his businesses were doing so well that he did not have to work. He and Debbie would have gone on the trip to Italy with their friends and had almost 10 years of their lives spent doing what they wanted to do. He would have also been able to build his business up enough to buy his own health insurance and would not have needed his employer to help pay for it.

For most people working a job, losing health insurance for their family can be almost a deal breaker. I have seen many people keep working well beyond retirement age because they need their employer to continue to pay for their health insurance. They are dependent on their job because they are unable to afford health insurance on their own.

It is very sad when someone works their entire life, beating up their body at a job, then being forced to continue working because of this.

Even before you quit your job, the best way to approach your health insurance is to look at it as a commodity. It's something that you can shop around for and hopefully get better prices with other companies. Just because your employer pays for a portion of your health insurance, you shouldn't automatically go with that insurance. The best time to plan for your health insurance is when you don't need it.

If you currently have a job where you use an employer based health insurance, you should work towards replacing it with your own insurance. By doing so, you are preparing yourself for your future without a job. Think of this as a problem that, as an entrepreneur, you need to solve. Try to find insurance that you can afford AND will take care of your needs. It may very well be that you are overpaying for your employer based health insurance and you could be saving lots of money by finding it on your own.

At the last job I ever had, my employer paid for a portion of my health insurance. It was decent insurance but for my family of six, our health insurance costs got up to $1,000 a month before I quit! That is a lot of money considering we are a young family and almost never go to the doctor. Even if I just stopped my insurance altogether and did not get any coverage, I would save $12,000 a year in costs, while saving that money for future medical expenses.

Three years before I quit my job, I got fed up with my employer based health insurance being so expensive. $12,000 a year was a lot of money and I figured there had to be a way to find something that would replace it. So, I started looking for health insurance outside of my job to compare the type of coverage and the costs associated with them.

In my search, I believed that I should at least get my health insurance costs cut in half by finding my own. All the health insurance companies were fighting for my business. I received many quotes from different companies and also looked to other types of health coverage. They were all comparable and were relatively the same price. Most were at least $300 cheaper than my current health insurance, so I believed I was on the right track.

After going through all of the big names in the business to find which were good and had much better rates for me, I found a company that fit my needs.

A Great Solution to the Health Insurance Problem

I approached this problem from all angles. Price, coverage, deductibles, premiums, reliability, etc. If you boil it all down, there are only two things you need to know about a potential insurance company.

1. How much money will come out of your pocket?
2. Will the insurance company pay your medical bills when you need them to?

Once I saw the problem in its simplest form, I was able to open my mind to other possibilities. There was no reason why I had to use the big-name companies anymore. My employers required me to use them because that is who they were contracted with. I, on the other hand, had no loyalties to any of these companies.

Then, one day I was listening to a radio station that only played Christian music and heard about a medical sharing program for Christians. The non-profit company I found was a medical sharing program called Medi-Share. This medical sharing program is not actually insurance, but handles all of my medical bills much like insurance, but is a fraction of the cost.

Basically, all of the people who participate in this program (220,000+ members) pool their money together, facilitated by the organization, and as anyone has a need, money is paid out for their health expenses. They cannot call themselves insurance because they are not an insurance company. The company is more of a community of people who have a common belief.

Since this is not actually insurance, the company does not act like an insurance company and thus does not make massive amounts of profits from its members. The money either goes to help those who are in need or help save people money with lower premiums and deductibles. My insurance expenses went from $1,000 a month to $200 a month by dropping my employer insurance and finding it on my own.

The Decision Made Easy

Because my family and I never go the doctor, I looked into a high deductible plan that took the least amount of money from my pocket each month. With my employer, I was paying $1000 a month and the high deductible plan with Medi-Share was only $200 a month. That is an $800 savings each month that would normally go to the insurance company. The big difference is that I have a high deductible of $10,000.

MY INSURANCE EXPENSES WENT FROM $1,000 A MONTH TO $200 A MONTH BY DROPPING MY EMPLOYER INSURANCE AND FINDING INSURANCE ON MY OWN.

So, on top of my $200 a month that I pay in premiums to the company, I pay all my medical expenses up to $10,000 for the entire household, and anything above that $10,000 the sharing program will cover. Since I and my family rarely ever go the doctor, I decided to take the "risk" of moving to this medical sharing program with a high deductible.

The great thing was that after one year of using Medi-Share, I would save $9,600 in insurance premiums from my employer based insurance. Since my deductible was $10,000, after one year I would have that entire deductible put away in savings ready for when I needed it. Year after year, I would continue to save close to $10,000 and put it into savings for the future.

When I finally quit my job, I had been on Medi-Share for over 3 years. That was $28,800 saved in just three years! That's almost $30,000 that would have gone to the insurance company, but is instead in my bank account earning interest for me.

Problem Solved.

TAKE ACTION

Find three insurance providers in your area that you can inquire about medical coverage: List them below:

Name: Phone #:

1. ____

2. ____

3. ____

Contact them and do some research. Write your notes on what these providers will cost monthly and what type of coverage they provide:

1. ____

____

____

2. ____

____

____

3. ____

____

____

Now, do more research to find which provider will best suit your needs. If it will help you, stop paying into your employer based insurance and start with your new insurance. Be sure to save that extra money in case you end up needing it for medical bills.

SECTION 3

C is for Capital Growth

"If you work just for money, you'll never make it, but if you love what you're doing and you always put the customer first, success will be yours."

– Ray Kroc

Cash is the lifeblood of your business. If you do not have cash, you and your business are finished. Just about every business problem can be solved with more cash. With more cash, you can hire more people, advertise more, hire lawyers, build buildings, etc. This is why a crucial component to your plan to quit your job is to increase your income as much as possible before you quit.

As I have said before, I want you to be able to afford everything you want. By building successful businesses, you will be able to do just that. While I recommend not spending wildly and having a budget, you should be able to have enough money to live the life you want to live. As you continue to build your business's earning capacity, you will have more money to fund your lifestyle.

For section 3, C stands for Capital Growth. This section is all about the capital (cash) in your businesses and to increase your income. Without income, your business dies and you are back to working a job. Before you quit your job, focus on growing the earning capacity of your business. The best answer to all of your business problems is...

MORE CASH!

CHAPTER TWELVE

LESSON 9

GROW YOUR BUSINESS BEFORE YOU QUIT

"Genius is one percent inspiration and ninety–nine percent perspiration."

– Thomas A. Edison

I made a huge mistake.

This was not one of those mistakes that you can just shrug off and move past quickly. No. This mistake cost me an entire year of my life.

Bills were piling up, money stopped coming in, and life was getting rough. My lovely wife had been concerned for a few months about how much money we were spending, but I didn't listen. I felt like I had everything figured out. I had built up my business enough to where I felt that the money would never stop coming in. The more money I made, the more money I spent, even when signs of trouble started popping up.

Taking expensive trips to private beach houses on the Pacific Ocean, buying awesome man-sized toys, lavish ski vacations, trips to Disneyland, taking the family on an amazing Hawaii vacation for 2 weeks, and even buying fantastic things like firearms, tools for my workshop, and many other fun, but not-so-necessary things. It seemed as though my businesses were going down fast and I was the one that caused it.

This mistake could have been prevented, but it added an entire year onto my plan to quit my job with passive income. I could have quit my job 1 year earlier than I did, but I took my eyes off the prize and became complacent. At year 7 of my 10-year plan, the passive income was rolling in well. So well in fact, that I started to spend the income from my passive income rather than invest it back into my business.

So, what was the mistake that made me quit my job one year later than I could have? The mistake was taking my eye off the prize of quitting my job. After many years of great success with my passive income businesses, I became complacent and did not continue building my business.

Feeling like I had enough money and it would never stop coming in, I would buy things I didn't need and spent most of that year's profits. Don't get me wrong, spending all that money was fun and enjoyable, but it does not compare to the fun and enjoyment of actually living a life without a job. I would gladly give back all the things that I purchased and all the things I did with that one year's profit in order to get one more year back of my life not working for somebody else.

What woke me up from that complacency was financially hard times. After spending the first seven months of profits from my businesses, I had three months of little to no income from my rental properties and other businesses. Instead of receiving $6000 or more a month from one area of the country I invested in, I received a fraction of the amount. Here is how the monthly checks came in the last half of the year:

- •July: $5384
- •August: $296
- •September: $384
- •October: $114
- •November $2167
- •December: $4591

NO MATTER HOW STRONG, PROFITABLE, OR EVEN BIG YOUR BUSINESS BECOMES, YOU CAN NEVER TAKE YOUR EYE OFF THE PRIZE OF BUILDING A BIGGER, STRONGER, AND MORE PROFITABLE COMPANY.

Adding insult to injury, spending much more money than I should have, I had many evictions, non-payments, and repairs needed for my rental properties. My monthly checks from the rental properties went from $6000 or more in positive cash flow a month to three months of negative income since I had mortgages, repairs, etc. that still needed to be paid.

Plus, all the money I spent were put on credit cards that came in the middle of the hard times. It was very difficult those months, to pay the entire balance off on the credit cards as I usually do every month. It was tough, but I forced myself to feel the pain of paying everything out of our emergency fund. There was no way I was going to pay any interest being stupid and borrowing too much money.

What I should have done was continue to keep my eye on the prize. My prize was to quit my job the fastest way possible. Spending the profit from my businesses really set me back. Looking back now I count that entire year almost as a lost year. If I had not become complacent but continued to build my business, I would have been able to quit my job in nine years rather than 10.

No matter how strong, profitable, or even big your business becomes, you can never take your eye off the prize of building a bigger, stronger, and more profitable company. This lesson has been so ingrained in me that even now after I quit my job, I'm even more focused on continually building my business and making even more money. I never want to fall into that same mistake again where I over spend and under earn.

Build, Build, Build

Just like that quote from the movie Tommy Boy, "Your business is either growing or dying. There ain't no third direction."

Continue to build and grow your businesses before you quit your job. Learn from my mistake and do not take your eye off the prize. When you spend the profits from your business on things you do not need, you delay your reward of being freed from a job.

The income your business creates must be invested back into the business. This reinvestment accelerates your goal of quitting your job. My original plan was to quit my job in 10 years. Even though it only took me nine years to do it, I would have done it in eight years had I continued to build the business. Now that I have already quit my job, I can tell you that life without a job is so much more amazing than you can even imagine. I thought I knew what it would be like to not have a job because I would take long vacations of four weeks or more but that does not even compare.

Until you actually quit your job, you will not know what it truly feels like to be free. A vacation from your job is just a taste or a glimpse of the reality. The reality is so much more profound because there is no longer a nagging feeling in the back of your mind that there's something that you should be doing at your job. Or that your vacation will end and the drudgery of your job will continue and you will be right back to where you started.

So, keep your eye on the prize. Learn from my mistake of being complacent to continually build your business every day. The joy of not having a job is absolutely worth it in the end.

TAKE ACTION

Name three ways you can grow your business in the next 12 months.

1. ____________________
2. ____________________
3. ____________________

What problems do you see that may hinder you from implementing these three items?

1. ____________________
2. ____________________
3. ____________________
4. ____________________
5. ____________________

What destructive habits/actions do you need to remove from your life in order for you to fully grow your business and accomplish your goals? List them below and what you will do to remove them:

____

____

____

____

____

____

CHAPTER THIRTEEN

LESSON 10

ADD ANOTHER STREAM OF INCOME BEFORE YOU QUIT

"Business opportunities are like buses, there's always another one coming."

– Richard Branson

"Honey, we just made an extra $1500 this month!" I shouted to my wife with excitement.

"How did we do that?" She asked.

"Our books that we have been selling online and have been doing terrific! It has also been very rewarding teaching so many people about passive income and helping them change their life for the better." I explained.

"And you just quit your job! Praise the Lord!" She said.

For the previous eight years, I had been working hard helping many other people invest in rental properties just like I have done. Most of these are either friends or coworkers that I shared my business with as I continued to build that over the years. Many of them began follow my lead and have done a terrific job building up their businesses too.

I have taught so many people how to invest in real estate and other businesses that I realized I should create another business teaching people the same thing. Along with the knowledge and ability to invest, I also have the passion to teach other people and get excited when others succeed. That is when I decided to create another business called Master Passive Income. This would be a new way for me to help people and create income for my family.

YOU WILL FIND THAT ONCE YOU QUIT YOUR JOB AND HAVE 40+ HOURS OF YOUR LIFE BACK, YOU WILL HAVE MUCH MORE TIME TO DEVOTE TO YOUR BUSINESSES.

My very first book "How to Quit Your Job with Rental Properties - A Step-By-Step Guide to Investing in Real Estate with Passive Income", was a culmination of all the years spent answering questions from new investors on how to do just what I've done. This book and two others that I wrote continually bring in money for my family every month. After I quit my job, I continued, and still continue, to build my business into a business of helping others.

With my rental property business, I only spend roughly 3 hours a month working on the business. This is because I pay property managers, inspectors, realtors, contractors, and other people to work on my business while I have the rest of my life to do what I want to do. I spend much more time devoted to helping people learn how to create passive income and quit their jobs with businesses.

Whatever your business is, be on the lookout for opportunities to create other streams of income for you and your family. You will find that once you quit your job and have 40+ hours of your life back, you will have much more time to devote to your businesses. Start today with building other businesses.

Once you are two or three years away from quitting your job with your first business, be on the lookout for new streams of income that will help you quit even sooner than you had planned.

Increase Your Income

In my book, "How to Quit Your Job with Passive Income - The Ultimate Beginners Guide to Wealth and Riches with 12 Proven Businesses You Can Start Today," I explained how you can add many other streams of income to your existing businesses. Each of these businesses is a passive income business that will make money even when you are not working. This is my favorite way to make money.

You don't need to live off one type of passive income for the rest of your life. Now that you will have 40+ hours to work on other passive income ideas every week, you will be able to bring in new streams of income.

Here is a quick (non-exhaustive) list of things you can do:

Write and Self Publish a Book Online

What are you passionate about? What do you know more than the average person about? What excites you? Do you have a story to tell that will entertain many people? Publishing a book is a tremendous way to get your message out to the world.

Create an Online Course

Are you good at math? Are you good at playing an instrument? There are many people who will pay you to learn how to do what you're accomplished at?

There are a few things you need to do.

1. Find what you want to teach.
2. Make sure there is a market.
3. Find the people who are in that market.
4. Create the online course.
5. Sell it to your market.

You can find lots of resource online on how to create and make money from an online course. Think about what you are good at and teach it!

Create a Blog

Just like the online course, what are you good at? What would people want to learn from you?

Maybe underwater sign language is something people want to learn about. I'm mostly joking but who knows, it may be a thing. Well, just set up a hosting account with bluehost.com and create a WordPress site with the name www.underwatersignlanguage.com and you are ready to blog.

You can start a blog in 4 minutes or less using bluehost.com.

BlueHost.com will walk you through everything from beginning to end. Once you sign up, you will have an account where you can set up your WordPress site and start blogging.

Affiliate Marketing

The link above for bluehost.com sends you to Blue Host through my affiliate. It gives me credit for referring you to them. Each time someone signs up through my link, I get a kickback from them. Most online companies have an affiliate program like this, and its setup to get more customers. When you drive people to their offering, you receive a small payment in return. The company's goal is to get more customers, and this is a cost-effective way to do that.

Plus, it doesn't cost the customer anything additional, and they often get a discount for signing up. For a thank you, when you refer a customer to them, they give you a kickback that doesn't even cost the customer anything.

The company saves money on marketing and gets a customer, the customer gets a product they need usually at a discount, and you make money.

So, it's a win-win-win all around.

Quick Example List of Other Business Ideas:

- Carpet Cleaning Business
- Handyman
- Tutor or Mobile Teacher
- Landscaper
- Event or Party Planner
- Consultant for Your Specialized Knowledge
- Personal Training
- Computer Repair
- Virtual Assistant
- Freelance Writer
- Copywriter
- Dog Trainer

TAKE ACTION

What other entrepreneurial ventures have you been considering or should consider before you quit your job? Write them in order below:

1. ______________________________

2. ______________________________

3. ______________________________

What is stopping you from adding these new streams of income?

1. ______________________________

2. ______________________________

3. ______________________________

4. ______________________________

5. ______________________________

What would you do right now to make more money if you did not have your job and had 40+ extra hours a week to devote to making money? Brainstorm your ideas below:

____

____

____

____

____

____

____

CHAPTER FOURTEEN

LESSON 11

FIND NEW WAYS TO SOLVE YOUR PROBLEMS AND MAKE EVEN MORE MONEY

"Even if you are on the right track, You'll get run over if you just sit there."

– Will Rogers

There is only one good benefit to having a job. That is a steady paycheck. It's a very nice thing to look in your checking account and find that a new sum of money has been deposited. Like clockwork, this same amount of money will be deposited the following two weeks and then again in two weeks. There is something very reassuring knowing that money will continuously be given to you each and every pay period. A steady paycheck allows you to have enough money to pay your bills, mortgage, and other expenses.

Without having a job, your income changes from a continual payment of the same amount to a varied payment of random amounts. Depending on the type of business you have, your income can come in monthly, weekly, or even daily. Also, those payments are usually never the same. After you quit your job, your income can, and will, go up and down depending on how well your business does that month.

Once you leave your job, you leave your steady income. With a rental property business, income fluctuates on a month-to-month basis with evictions, repairs, nonpayment etc. Being an entrepreneur though, taking the risk of leaving a steady paycheck for freedom without a job is worth it. The trick is to make your business income as stable as possible.

A Surprising Answer to a Huge Problem

I was desperate. What else was I going to do?

Money was flowing out of my pocket. So many things were going wrong. I couldn't keep a tenant, thieves broke in and stole the furnace, broke in again to steal the hot water heaters, then again to steal the copper plumbing. Taxes, fees, and other expenses were taking money from me left and right. The properties were making my stomach turn, almost making me sick.

Finally, I decided the only way to get rid of this problem was to get rid of the property. I knew I had to sell the property and sell it fast. The property was listed for sale, and had absolutely no interest from any potential buyers. The home attracted only one buyer after three months on the market. Their offer almost offended me. Granted, it was a very old home that needed a lot of work but the offer was 1/4 what I paid for it. I felt so desperate that I almost took it the offer.

While I was considering the offer, I received a call from a different potential buyer. He had found me through my listing on Craigslist.com.

"Hi, I'm interested in your property. Are you willing to sell it with a land contract or rent to own?" Steven asked.

This question had me perplexed. I would usually answer these types of questions with a quick "No" and move on. This time, I considered it. After months on the market, what could I lose? The reason why I usually said no was that I would eventually have to turn the property over to the renter and not own the property any more. This time, I would be happy to no longer own this particular property.

"Yes, I am open to it. Let me get back to you on the terms of the rent-to-own," I said as thoughts ran through my head.

This one area of the country that I invest in, a lot of the properties are very old and needed lots of repairs, maintenance, and updates every month. Along with those expenses, tenants would come and go frequently. My monthly cash flow of income only stabilizes when tenants stay in the property for longer periods of time. This has the added benefit of reducing the repairs and maintenance.

Let me pause the story for a bit and give you some context to my problem. For one year prior to quitting my job, I focused hard on being proactive in the repairs and maintenance of my properties. I repaired or replaced furnaces, roofs, re-painted walls, repaired plumbing, and took care of many other deferred maintenance items. Along with those, I was much more selective in finding the best possible tenants for the property who would not move out quickly.

Even after doing all this, I was still having a hard time keeping good paying tenants who would take care of the property. It was about this time that I decided to sell the property and move my money over to another part of the country that would likely be a better investment. For my family, I needed stable income each month to provide for our needs.

Back to the story.

Remember how I explained that entrepreneurs are problem solvers? Well, my big problem was with a certain ZIP Code where some of my properties were located. It had a high eviction and turnover rate along with high expenses. It seemed as though I was evicting tenants every eight months. With eviction fees, lawyer fees, cleaning fees, and carrying costs, an eviction can cost up to $1500 for one property. Any one eviction could eat up half of your entire year's profits for the property.

My problem was three-fold:

1. Tenant evictions and vacancies took lots of time and money.
2. These older properties (100+ years old) cost a lot of money in maintenance and repairs.
3. Moving the money invested in these properties to another, better property, would be a wise choice.

These three problems needed to be addressed before I could quit my job. Only with stable, consistent income would I be able to rely on my investments and quit my job. I found two ways to solve the problem.

One was to have my properties rented to section 8 tenants. This is a government-funded program helping low-income families with a place to live by giving them money for rent each month. There are many hurdles the owner must jump through in order to have a section 8 property approved by the government. But, once you have the necessary repairs done to the property, tenants stay and the money keeps rolling in.

I have a number of properties that are section 8 and they are doing fantastic. Section 8 tenants rarely ever move and the government never misses a payment. This solution helped solved one of the three problems I had regarding high turnover of tenants. There were two problems that needed to be addressed as well. For the properties that were not able to be in the section 8 program, I found a solution that answered all three problems these properties brought.

The Win-Win Solution

Business is more than just making money. It is about people. In your business, if you focus on helping people, you create win-win solutions that benefit everyone. Instead of focusing on profits, focus on what you can do for your customers and how you can bring them the best value.

> BUSINESS IS MORE THAN JUST MAKING MONEY. IT IS ABOUT PEOPLE. IN YOUR BUSINESS, IF YOU FOCUS ON HELPING PEOPLE, YOU CREATE WIN-WIN SOLUTIONS THAT BENEFIT EVERYONE.

The second solution I found actually answered all three of my problems. The solution was to create a rent-to-own program. This program will allow a tenant the ability to own the house in 10 years, as long as they make their monthly payment and maintain the property. This basically made me the bank for many potential homeowners. This solved the three problems for me AND blessed a family with the ability to own a home in 10 years.

Here are the current terms for these homes in this one particular area:

- $1,500 down payment (non-refundable).
- $495 a month rent.
- $495 security deposit.
    - Total to move in: $2,490.
    - I quit claim the deed into their name in 10 years if they follow the lease and contract.
    - After 10 years, they own the home.

- I make $60,000 over the course of 10 years for a property that I couldn't even sell for $9,000.
- All maintenance and expenses are paid for by the tenants.

With the rent-to-own deal I have in place for my tenants, they are responsible for every aspect of the house. Repairs, maintenance, upgrades, and all other expenses are to be paid by them. I tell all of them to think of me as a bank and to not call me if there are any issues with the house. It is now their responsibility to maintain and repair the property due to the terms of the agreement. They will soon be the new owners of the property with a loan from me to buy the property. With the rent-to-own program, the tenants are fully invested into the property because of their $1,500 down payment and their ability to own a home in 10 years.

This is a huge WIN-WIN for everyone involved. The tenants would never have enough money to buy a home and I have given them the ability to do so. They take pride in ownership of their home and will take care of it better than any tenant would. Now my income is stable AND I have no more expenses.

WINNING!

Whatever your business is, it is crucial that you solve the problem of fluctuating income on a month-to-month basis.

TAKE ACTION

What is keeping you from making even more money in your business? Write the reasons below:

1. ____

2. ____

3. ____

What win-win solutions can you think of that will help you to solve these problems and make even more money?

1. ____

2. ____

3. ____

4. ____

5. ____

Being an entrepreneur is all about solving problems and never giving up. Find problems you can solve that are keeping you from making even more money from other businesses and brainstorm how you can get through these roadblocks:

____

____

____

____

____

____

____

CHAPTER FIFTEEN

LESSON 12

GET ALL THE FINANCING YOU NEED BEFORE YOU QUIT

"If you would like to know the value of money, try to borrow some."

– Benjamin Franklin

$100,000 was practically burning a hole in my pocket and I couldn't spend it fast enough.

The more I looked for something to spend all that cash on, the more it seemed like I would never be able to do it. As impatience started to creep in all over me, I saw my plans slipping away.

My time was running out. If I didn't spend this money in the next few weeks, it would all be over. In just three more weeks, I would blow right past my time-line and I would be stuck with the money. This was another problem for me. Yes, this is a good problem to have, but not one that I wanted.

For five months, I had been looking for another property to invest in. With my rental property business, I had a special process for recycling money over and over again, building my rental portfolio bigger and bigger.

Having money to buy more income producing properties is crucial. 9 years ago, I did this same process for the very first time. This simple process has a simple name to it. The B.R.R.R.R. Strategy. This strategy is where you Buy, Rehab, Rent, Refinance, Repeat." As simple as it sounds, it is a long and involved process, but has really advanced my rental property business over the years.

Basically, I buy a rental property for cash. Then I rehab/fix up the property to make it rent-ready. Once it is fixed up, I have my property manager find and place a good tenant into it. When the property is producing a monthly cash flow, I refinance the property with a bank and pull out ALL the money I invested into it. This process basically allows me to own a property with almost NO money of my own put into the property. Since I pull out all my money, I am free to do with it whatever I want.

With the refinance of the property, I proceed to purchase another rental property with the ability to repeat the process all over again. Each time I repeat this process, my business grows, I make more money, and I own more real estate increasing my net worth.

Like I said, this process is much more complicated than it sounds. If you want to know more about it, you can see it on my website at: http://www.masterpassiveincome.com/brrrr

If I didn't spend the $100,000 in the next few weeks, my window to accomplish this B.R.R.R.R. plan one more time before I quit my job would be closed. My plan was to quit in December 2016, and I hadn't even started the first part of the process, let alone the refinance portion. My ability to refinance these properties and get my money out of them was going away quickly. Banks do not like it when someone quits their job in the middle of a refinancing process. For some reason, they don't think the loan would be paid back (*insert sarcasm*).

Over the course of the two months, I purchased four properties for a total of $100,000 in cash. The beautiful thing is that these four properties bring in a total of $3000 in cash flow into my pocket each month. Once I had these properties in my possession, I wasted no time and started the refinance process immediately. Even though two were not rented yet, I still wanted the long refinance process to be finished quickly.

"OK Mr. Heiner, your loan has been funded. Your bank should receive the wire transfer in a couple hours." My loan broker informed me over the phone.

"Terrific, I really appreciate the help with this entire process. The three months of waiting for this finally paid off," I said.

The reality was, even though I could barely stand my job anymore, I couldn't quit until the process was finished. After a long couple of months in the loan process, the wire transfer for $78,791.44 was deposited into my account on January 3rd 2017. With this new money in my account, I was able to purchase more properties which would make me even more money.

AS I STATED MANY TIMES, BANKS DO NOT LIKE IT WHEN YOU QUIT YOUR JOB IN THE MIDDLE OF GETTING A LOAN.

Finance or Refinance Everything

As I stated many times, banks do not like it when you quit your job in the middle of getting a loan. Their entire business plan is to lend money to people who will pay them back with interest. They make sure each person they give a loan to is more than likely going to fulfill their obligation to pay off the debt.

If you are in my line of work and need to refinance properties, do it before you quit. Once you do, you no longer have that income and may not be able to show the bank you have enough income to pay the debt. Banks require your debt to income ratio be at a certain level for the lender to feel comfortable lending their money to you.

What about if you want to purchase a new vehicle or buy yourself a jet-ski? In order to finance a big purchase like this, it is much easier to get the loan if you can show the bank you have income from your job as a source to repay the loan.

Now that you see the value of a job to get a loan, think about the loans you already have. I suggest you look at ALL your loans to see if you should refinance any of them. You could get a lower rate, shorter term length, or find a way to pull money out and use it to make more money. Go through all your loans and make sure they are the best rates and terms for you and your family. If the rates can be lowered enough to make it a good investment, be sure to finish the refinance before you quit your job.

In the end, make sure you do not need to have any more banks verify your income and ability to repay the loan after you quit.

SECTION 4

H is for Hacking Your Future

"You were born to win, but to be a winner, you must plan to win, prepare to win, and expect to win."

~ Zig Ziglar

My wife and I have four terrific children. They are truly a blessing.

When my wife told me she was pregnant with our first child, my mind went 100mph thinking of all the problems, issues, and worries that come with having a child. Many feelings came over me almost all at once. I felt I wasn't prepared, didn't know what I was going to do, or even that I would screw everything up for my family. Even though I had all these emotions crashing over me, month after month my worries slowly went away. It was as if the Lord God made child baring take 9 months just to help parents adjust to life with a child.

Going from having a job to being an entrepreneur is not much different than this. For the longest time, all you know is life with a job. Year after year, you become comfortable and complacent. Then you start a business and build it year after year. When your business is finally ready to be your only source of income, the countdown begins. Just like the nine months of pregnancy, you have to give yourself a time limit to quit your job.

My business was built up enough for me to quit my job 12 months before I actually did. I knew I was ready to quit my job but I didn't have the conviction to do it. So, I gave myself a deadline. I told myself I had 12 months to prepare for life without a job. Just 12 more months receiving a steady paycheck, and then I will make myself quit. From that time on, the deadline forced me to focus my efforts on only the most important things that would help me be successful in the months and years without a job.

In those 12 months, if I had a concern or worry about the future, I counted it as a problem to solve, not something that would hold me back. Being proactive and planning for your future without a job is the best way to set yourself up for success. What if you could give yourself a head start now and plan your future to be an absolute success when you quit your job? Wouldn't you take it? I sure would, and did.

In this section, we will look at how to be as prepared as possible for life without a job and a steady paycheck. The year leading up to when I quit my job, I was very worried about not being able to rely on that consistent income from my paycheck. I began to question myself thinking my business was not good enough or that I would fail and my family would end up on the streets. Thinking through all the potential issues and problems that may arise, I was able to set myself up for success.

For section 4, **H is for Hacking Your Future.** Savings, expenses, income, financing, etc. are all items in your future that have to be rethought. Life with a steady paycheck is almost over and now it is crucial to plan how to quit successfully. Issues may arise like, your business is not doing well, or if you need financing to fund your business. These possibilities and more need to be taken into account before you quit your job.

Your future is what you make it. Time to start hacking it so you can be successful without that job that is holding you back from life.

CHAPTER SIXTEEN

LESSON 13

LIVING ON YOUR BUSINESS INCOME WITHOUT YOUR JOB

"People become really quite remarkable when they start thinking that they can do things. When they believe in themselves, they have the first secret of success."

~ Norman Vincent Peale

I was terrified the first time I did it.

Even though we had a plan, we didn't have a plan B. Plan A seemed possible but highly unlikely that we would actually pull it off and be successful. The baby was coming in 9 months, ready or not.

Our first child was a beautiful baby girl who made life so fun.

With all that fun came a dramatic loss of income. Not just the loss of income from my wife no longer working but all the new expenses that come with a baby. Diapers, food, clothing, and more were expenses we now had to account for.

While Melissa and I were engaged, we both decided she would stay at home and raise our children while I worked. It was not just being home as they grew older while they went through government school, she had a strong desire to homeschool them as well. We believed, and still do, that it would be best for her to be the one to teach our children. Now, much further along in life with four children, we are very glad and know that we made the right decision for our family.

For many years, she had her own job and made decent money. When we opened our retail location, she quit her job to manage the store. Day in and day out, she worked hard managing the employees, inventory, handling sales, and everything a manager needed to do to run a business. This went on for a year or so. Then she got pregnant. Knowing that she was not going to continue working and earning a paycheck, we needed a plan for the future with only one income.

Many questions came into our minds:

"Would we have enough money to pay our mortgage?"

"Will our insurance cover everything?"

"Do we have enough savings?"

"Should we give up a stable job for something we believe is better?"

Even though all these questions and thoughts were running through our minds, we knew it was the right decision. No matter what, we would make it work. Looking back now, years later, we have never regretted a minute of her not working. There were some sacrifices in our lives that we had to make along the way, but it was all worth it.

No one ever said on their deathbed, "I wish I would have worked more hours at my job." My wife and I whole-heartedly agree with that sentiment.

Living on your business income is a leap of faith.

There are some financial preparations you need to think through, and plan for, before you stop working. Though it can be done, it wouldn't be very wise to just up and quit without having things like savings, a budget, and a plan for life without a steady paycheck. Most people do not want to take the risk of living one income, let alone living solely on their business income. This lesson will help you think through this process before you quit.

Analyze Your Expenses

A few years ago, there was a financial "Guru" that was teaching people his way of being rich. A term he coined was called the "Latte Factor." As this guru went through his lesson, he pointed out one person who had a latte from a local coffee shop. From there, he went on a 10-minute explanation of how much that person was spending each week, month, and year on their latte's. Hence the name, "Latte Factor."

As he went through the numbers, $5 a day times, 5 days a week, multiplied by 52 weeks a year, adds up to $1,300 a year spent on fancy coffee. Now, I will say that I completely agree with the premise he is making. Little expenses add up to be big expenses in the end. That being said, his teaching was basically how to work a job until retirement, stop spending, save your money, and have a large bank account when you retire. These ideas are not bad in and of themselves, but I believe they miss the mark when it comes to actually building wealth.

Here are a few huge problems I see with that type of thinking:

1. You don't know if your money will last the rest of your life.

2. You don't know if you will live to retirement age.
3. Your prime years in life are spent working for someone else.
4. Your money is not working for you but just sitting there in a bank earning .0015% interest.
5. You are passing up the finer things in life in the hopes that you will enjoy them when you are 68 or older.

Personally, I do not want to wait until I am 68 years old to enjoy my money, let alone my life. At the time of my writing this, I have already quit my job and I am only 37 years old. If I waited until I was 68 years old, that would be another 31 years before I could actually live my life.

If you want to have a latte every day, you should work to build a business that will pay for your lattes. If you want to be able to ski for 1 month a year in Whistler, British Columbia, then you should focus on making enough money from your businesses to pay for it. Missing out on things you desire is not the goal. Earning enough money to pay for those things is the goal.

NO MATTER IF YOU BELIEVE YOU ARE PAYING THE LOWEST AMOUNT POSSIBLE, THERE CAN STILL BE A WAY TO REDUCE YOUR EXPENSES EVEN FURTHER.

Even though we are all about making money to pay for the things we want, it is also wise to make sure you are not spending any more than you absolutely have to. This leads me to another business lesson I learned from owning my business, Downtown Express.

Your expenses can always be reduced.

No matter if you believe you are paying the lowest amount possible, there can still be a way to reduce your expenses even further. When I set up the business, I found the best and least expensive credit card processor out there at the time. Four years later, the new owner of the business found a new credit card processor who charged them half as much as I was being charged. As times change, so do prices.

Always be looking for ways to cut your expenses. Even if you believe you have already found the best and least expensive service possible.

Cut and/or Reduce Your Expenses

Now that you have one income and a budget, it is time for you to find all expenses that you can cut or reduce. I will say that life is not about going without the good things in life. You should be able to do what you want, when you want to do it.

Having a $5 latte each day is not bad in and of itself, but can be if you do not have the money to buy it. Enjoying the finer things in life is what being an entrepreneur allows you to do. If you have the money and put it in your budget, spend away. Just make sure you do not spend money you do not have.

This exercise is about cutting expenses, not cutting out the things you want. Look at every way you can to reduce how much you spend on the things you already receive. Do you need that NFL Package with your cable television subscription? How about that cable package itself while we are at it? Do you NEED that?

I'm not saying that YOU don't need these. I'm merely asking the question for you to consider for yourself if you really need/want them. Consider all of your expenses to make sure these are the things you want to spend your money on.

I suggest calling every company you get services from and ask to have your rates reduced or even cut.

Here is a quick list to get you started:

- Credit cards interest rates

- Cell phones plans
- Cable TV or satellite service
- Gym memberships
- Pest control
- Yard service
- Home internet service
- Home insurance rates
- Automobile insurance
- Home security monitoring system

For example, I once cut my satellite TV bill from $80 a month to $11 just by asking. My family and I never really watched TV very much, so I decided to call and cancel my subscription. While talking with the service provider about canceling, they asked why I wanted to cancel. After informing them that we just did not watch it and didn't want to spend the money anymore, the service person asked me what it would take to keep our business.

Wow, great question, I thought. After thinking about it for a second, I told her I didn't want to pay $80 anymore and to just cancel the service. She then asked, how much would you be willing to pay to keep the service? I said, "$10". Even though I did want to cancel, $10 a month would be just low enough that I would continue with the service. A few minutes later, she worked her magic and now my bill for the service is $11 a month!

For the better part of two years, my TV service has been $11.14 a month with HD, DVR, 90 channels, etc. WINNING!

Here are other ways you can cut costs and save money:

- Buy food in bulk from places like Costco.
- Dried and frozen food is inexpensive and lasts a long time.

- Sell the expensive car you have and buy an old beater car for a fraction of the price.
- Use GasBuddy.com to find cheaper gas.
- Maybe find a smaller home to live in and rent out your large home to someone who wants to spend all that money.
- Cut luxuries you don't need. Haircuts, manicures, etc.
- Eat at home more often. You pay at least twice as much to eat out than you would if you ate at home.

Remember, this exercise is to reduce your expenses so your money will go further each month without your paycheck. There is no need to pay a penny more for the goods and services than you have to.

THE DIFFERENCE BETWEEN EARNING AND MAKING IS, AS A BUSINESS OWNER, YOU MAKE MONEY FROM PLACES WHERE IT DOESN'T ALREADY EXIST.

Afford Everything

A quick sidebar about income and expenses.

As I said before, having a business is all about making money, not earning it. The difference between earning and making is, as a business owner, you make money from places where it doesn't already exist. Before you created your business, that specific stream of income wasn't there for you. The money was already in the pockets of your customers, you just didn't have a way to transfer it to you. When you are an employee, your boss already has the money and agrees to give it to you when you give him your time.

With a job, you earn money. With a business, you make money. The goal of your businesses is to be able to live however YOU want to live. Not how someone else tells you to live. If you want to buy a Ferrari, build your business big enough to afford it. If you want to travel the world, you design your business so that you can be anywhere in the world and still conduct your business remotely. With your business, you will have the time and money to afford the trip.

In your business, the only thing holding you back is yourself. As you continue to build your business and increase your income, you have the ability to make enough money to afford anything you want. The more effort, planning, and execution you put into your business properly, the more your business will grow. Again, the only limitation is you and what you are capable of achieving.

Do you think Warren Buffet, Bill Gates, or Donald Trump have a spending budget for themselves? I am not sure if they do or not, but a safe guess is that they make so much money that they don't need a budget any more. They probably make enough in one month to cover their year of expenses. Your goal is to build your businesses enough so that you no longer need a budget because you have so much money coming in.

As In Everything, Practice Makes Perfect!

The best way to know if you can live on your business income is to just do it. I suggest that you start living on your business income one year before you actually quit your job. Since you still have your job, you have the ability to give it a trial run to see what it is like. Doing this will allow you to know what your income and expenses will be like when you quit.

A great way to do this is to create a new bank account that is completely separate from the accounts you already have. Once that is open, have your entire paycheck taken out of your account every month and deposit it into this new account. Set it aside and don't touch it, even if life gets rough. Dip into your savings if you have to, but leave your job income alone in this new bank account. Do this for a minimum of 6 months to really see the ups and downs that one income will bring.

A huge side bonus of doing this is that after 6 months, you will have your entire income saved for when you no longer have a job. If you make $60,000 a year from your job, you could have saved close to $30,000 in your trial run by saving your income. If you did this for the entire year, you will have $60,000 saved as an emergency fund for the ups and downs of your business and life.

Living on your business income is absolutely possible.

Trust me.

TAKE ACTION

How much money do you need monthly to live on if you quit your job? Use the Quick Budget Calculator to find the numbers below:

Download it here: http://www.masterpassiveincome.com/quickbudget

Total Potential Business Income: $_______________________

Total Expenses: $_______________________

Total Difference: $_______________________

If the difference is negative then you will lose money each month.

How much money can you save each month from your job to practice living on your business income?

Total Monthly Saved from Paycheck: $_______________________

Total Months Until You Quit: _______________________

Total Saved ($ saved x months): $_______________________

What expenses can you cut out completely or reduce now in preparation for living on one income?

1. ____
2. ____
3. ____
4. ____
5. ____

Start today with reducing your expenses.

CHAPTER SEVENTEEN

LESSON 14

PESSIMISM IS GOOD WHEN IT COMES TO FUTURE INCOME

"Capital isn't scarce; vision is."

- Sam Walton

I was forced to do it. What else could I do?

My business partners were fed up, minimum wage had gone up 15% two times in two years, sales had been declining since the real estate market crash of 2009, and money was running out. All eyes were focused on me as we met together for our monthly business meeting. The question in their eyes were all the same: "What are we going to do?"

Four years before, we had high hopes and dreams that this little business would grow to be a large business with multiple locations. The business was called Downtown Express and we built it from the ground up. Literally. The location of the business was a building that did not have a concrete slab, plumbing, electrical, etc. The concept, design, and functionality were all created by my partners and I. We worked for months building, designing, and developing the business to be as successful as possible. We all believed that this business would allow us to quit our jobs while continuing to build the business year after year.

"Sales are just not what they were before the real estate market crash. People all around us lost their jobs and our customers do not have the money they did in the past" Sky, my business partner said.

"I know." I replied sadly.

"We need to sell the business while we can. The sales are still good enough for an owner/operator to buy it and make a good living. Why don't we try to sell the business?" Denise, another partner added.

"It is not like selling a car on Craigslist.com or even a house. There is much more that goes into it. Also, the amount of people looking for our type of business is very small. Maybe 1 in 1000 people or worse. There are not many people looking to buy a business let alone a retail store like ours, as well as desire this specific location." I interjected.

"Well, we need to do something. Soon we will be putting our own money into the business just to keep it open. We don't want to do that. We would rather close up the business than do that." Sky stated.

Being the perpetual optimist, I said to them: "Alright, I will find a buyer. I will get us out of this."

This was supposed to be our ticket out of our jobs. It was a good deal, but had become an ordeal, and now my partners wanted a new deal. This business was my idea from the beginning and I was the CEO of the company. I took it upon myself to find a buyer for the business, as futile as it would be.

Three months later, after trying everything to find a buyer and failing, I couldn't help but beat my head with this one question: "Why did I tell them I could sell the business?" Now that I had promised the business would be sold, it was up to me to figure out how to do it. As an entrepreneur, this was a problem that I had to solve. It was not just me on the line, it was my business partners as well.

Two months later, on December 31st 2010, I successfully sold the business. After all was said and done, we did lose money on the sale of the business from what we put into it. That hurt. The bright side was that we were no longer on responsible for the lease which had another two years left. We were completely out of a business that was costing us money every day.

WHATEVER YOUR PROFIT PROJECTIONS ARE, CUT THEM IN HALF. IF YOU CAN SURVIVE WITH THAT, THEN YOU HAVE A GOOD CHANCE.

A Lesson Learned

Looking back now, it is easy to see how we could have been better at figuring out our income and expenses. One lesson I took away from this business experience was: Whatever your profit projections are, cut them in half. If you can survive with that, then you have a good chance. For me, this applies to all types of businesses. Especially the businesses that you depend on to pay your bills when you quit your job.

I was created as an eternal optimist. It takes a lot for me to be pessimistic in anything. Actually, there is a song that really explains me. (possibly to a fault) The 1946 Broadway musical "Annie Get Your Gun" has Annie and Frank battle back and forth in a song who can do things better than the other. The song is affectionately called "Anything You Can Do".

During the song, Frank and Annie playfully argue about who can be better than the other in many different things. Sing softly, sing higher, sing sweeter, hold a note longer, etc. The main line that resonates with me is "Anything you can do, I can do better."

Maybe it is the entrepreneur in me, but that is usually how I view the world and everything in it. Where someone else failed, I will succeed. Where someone else succeeded, I can do it better than them. Yes, I know it is not totally true, but because I am an entrepreneur, I am driven to succeed, no matter what.

Now, in the area of income, I focus on being pessimistic. Selling my business was a hard lesson to learn, but I did. When it came time to quit my job, I knew that I needed to account for the possibility that my income from my businesses would not come in as I projected. My expenses don't really change much (unless I do something out of the ordinary). The bills come in each month whether I have money to pay them or not.

This is why it is best to plan your income, but be pessimistic on the total amount you can bring in. For example, if my rental property business usually makes $10,000 a month or more then I need to be pessimistic and cut that in half. If I can survive on $5,000 a month and still pay all my bills and expenses, then I figure I will be just fine.

Remember my story where I had three months of no income from my businesses, but still had expenses and was buying things I did not need? Yeah, that was pretty bad. Times will come where you have ups and downs in your business. Make sure that when those low-income months come you have already accounted for the lack in income because you were pessimistic about your income.

TAKE ACTION

What do you expect your monthly income to be in each of the next six months? Write them in below:

Month 1: $______________________________

Month 2: $______________________________

Month 3: $______________________________

Month 4: $______________________________

Month 5: $______________________________

Month 6: $______________________________

Potential Six Month Income: $_________________________

What were the previous six months income? Write them below:

Month 1: $______________________________

Month 2: $______________________________

Month 3: $______________________________

Month 4: $______________________________

Month 5: $______________________________

Month 6: $______________________________

Total Six Month Income: $_________________________

Are your future projections for your business realistic compared to how your previous six months really were?

How will you proceed given any issues with past and future expected income? Brainstorm your solutions below.

____

____

____

CHAPTER EIGHTEEN

LESSON 15

WHAT AN ACCOUNTANT SAYS ABOUT QUITTING YOUR JOB

"Twenty years from now you will be more disappointed by the things that you didn't do than by the ones you did do."

~ Mark Twain

I failed the first time I tried it.

It didn't help that I didn't really put all my effort into it. Maybe it was a lack of passion, drive, or even desire, but ability wasn't the problem. I had succeeded in tougher things in the past. I had accomplished many difficult things in my lifetime: walking on and making the Fresno State University football team, starting a successful graphic and website design company; and a few others. These were great accomplishments for me. The reason why was because I had passion and a desire to be successful in those.

In this though, I failed. I received a "D" for my Accounting 4A class in college. A "D" Grade was not a passing grade and I would not graduate without passing this class. Trying again a second time, I didn't fare much better, but did eventually pass the class.

Accounting 4A and 4B were the required accounting classes I needed to graduate with a Bachelors in Business. Like most people, other than "bean counters" (Accountants), I hated the class. Even though I passed these classes, the real thing I learned from taking them was that I should pay someone else to do what I hated doing.

MY BUSINESS GROWS AS I FOCUS ON MY STRENGTHS TO BUILD THE BUSINESS.

Now, I know what you are thinking, and I didn't pay someone to take my tests and do my homework. I did however partner up with someone who loved the class and planned on being an accountant after college. She loved accounting and I hated it. There is nothing that puts me to sleep faster than a general ledger with its debits and credits boring me to death. Looking at a general ledger, I'd be out cold in 30 seconds flat and dead asleep.

As a business owner, I look at the profit and loss of a company or organization. That is where entrepreneurs know if their business is making money or not.

This experience in my college accounting course taught me the value of paying others, like accountants, to do what I do not want to do. They love doing the work, have a passion for numbers, and are great at what they do. What takes them 7 hours to do, would take me 7 weeks to do and I would HATE every minute of it.

Along with paying my accountant, there is another person I love to pay money to in this world. The managers of my rental properties. These wonderful people do all the things I could do, but would rather pay them to do it. I don't want to use my time cleaning up properties, finding tenants, collecting rents, and going through the hassle of evictions. Just like my accountant, my life is easier when I pay them to do the work I don't want to do.

Both my Property Managers and Accountants I work with make my life so much easier. My business grows as I focus on my strengths to build the business. Having enough money to pay these wonderful people is a problem that I am glad to find a solution for. I can afford good accountants because I spend my time where it is best used.

Time for a Sit-Down Conversation

Six months before I quit my job, I sat down with my accountant to see if there was anything I should prepare for before I quit. He's been in the business for many years and has even worked for the IRS so he knows how they work. Even better, he worked as an auditor for the IRS, so he has a good knowledge of how to stay away from being audited.

I spent over an hour with him running through my plan of quitting my job with passive income to get his wisdom and expertise. The very first thing that he said to me was, "Yes, you should absolutely quit your job!" This somewhat threw me off a little bit. I thought that maybe he would have been a bit more cautious or pessimistic about leaving a career. He wasn't though. He was very excited for me.

He quit his IRS job many years prior to this conversation. Before he quit is job to start his own private practice doing accounting and taxes, he said that many people were telling him he was crazy to leave a terrific job with the government. He was newly married, had a baby coming, and had a great job with great benefits. Now, decades later, he is very glad he became an entrepreneur and has never looked back.

Taxes

The IRS tax code is very complex and arduous for most people to understand. He shared about the tax implications of quitting my job. He told me about the tax code and how I could utilize it to benefit me in my business legally. Once I quit my job, I would be a "Real Estate Professional" which gave me a lot of new benefits in regards to my taxes.

A real estate professional status is based on how many hours you work doing real estate activities.

Becoming a qualified real estate professional, as deemed by the IRS, you can take an unlimited amount of real estate loss against your other income no matter how much money you make. If you are not a real estate professional, you can take a loss of up to $25,000 per year if you make less than $100,000. So, it's a much greater advantage to be a real estate professional because you can write off 100% of your real estate losses against your other income.

Having many rental properties with mortgages on them would be better than owning them outright, for tax purposes. He advised me that having your houses paid off is a great thing, but for tax purposes, a lot of money would be wasted on taxes. This is because I can write off all the mortgage interest that I pay to the bank. An easy way to understand it is that every PIG needs a PAL.

Every PIG needs a PAL

A PIG is an acronym for Passive Income Generator, and a PAL is a Passive Activity Loss.

What it boils down to is the IRS allows you to have deductions on your taxes. As an investor, having a mortgage on a property gives investors the ability to deduct all the interest charged for your mortgage. This is called "qualified residential mortgage interest". This is different than investment interest which I won't go into, but is heavily taxed.

A qualified residential mortgage interest allows you to write off the interest of your mortgages against your taxes as deductions. This lowers your taxable income which allows you to pay less in taxes. So, for every PIG (passive income generator - rental property) you need a PAL (passive activity loss - mortgage interest) which will help you offset your taxes.

I have written extensively on how to use financing to buy more properties AND make LOTS of money. If you look at the B.R.R.R.R. real estate technique of buying real estate, every property you have would have a mortgage on it.

B.R.R.R.R. = Buy, Rehab, Rent, Refinance, Repeat

There are many benefits of having a mortgage on the property.

1. The tenants will be paying all the interest and YOU get all the tax savings!
2. You take all the equity out of the property in the form of a loan and use that money to buy more houses.
3. The money taken out of the property is tax free!
4. Your business expands quickly because you are using other people's money. (O.P.M.)
5. The tenant is paying off the principal amount of the loan.

For real estate businesses, having a mortgage on a property will offset your taxes. The great thing is that your tenants are paying the interest for you in the form of their rent.

Financing of More Properties

A big concern of mine, and many others, was how I would get mortgages on properties if I did not have a W-2 from a job that shows stable income. Banks heavily rely on a W-2 from your job to prove your ability to repay back the lone. Obviously, they would be hard pressed to give you a loan if they think your income may not support the loan you are getting from them.

There was a way around it though and that is with good business income. My accountant went on to tell me that the banks will have to look at cash flow as well as your previous tax returns to show how much money you make. If your taxes reflect income enough to handle the new mortgage you are trying to acquire, lenders are willing to lend you the money for your next investment property. If not, they will not give you the loan because they don't think you can repay it.

SMALL LOCAL BANKS WOULD BE MORE INTERESTED IN YOUR BUSINESS THAN THE LARGE BANKS BECAUSE LARGER BANKS ARE CONCERNED ABOUT THE BIG DOLLAR CUSTOMERS.

A great suggestion my accountant had was to stay away from the large banks like Chase, Wells Fargo, and Bank of America. These banks are big and don't concern themselves with little guys. He recommended making relationships with small local banks. Local banks would be more interested in your business than the large banks because larger banks are concerned about the big dollar customers. The types of customers who are in the millions of dollars range.

A smaller bank would look at a smaller profitable business like mine more closely. After proving the business model, my historical income and expenses for the business, and my ability to repay the loan, they would most likely be willing to lend me the money. The banks love to give out loans, it is their lifeblood. The banks earn interest from the loans they give to customers. When it is all said and done though, expect to have a harder time getting financing on your properties.

Using Cash as Collateral

Another great idea was to take $100,000 of my own personal money and allow the bank to hold that as collateral and borrow against it. I can use the same $100,000 in collateral against multiple properties over and over again by putting them into a Certificate of Deposit at their institution. Every bank is different, so check with your local or preferred bank for their loan programs.

This could be a great way to purchase new properties and still have assets in the bank. Imagine being able to buy home after home with the same amount of money over and over again. I will say that I have not actually done this yet, so I can't really say how this would actually work. It does seem though to be a great thing to look into to build your business.

There were many other things that my accountant and I talked about, but these are the key takeaways from the meeting. The information I learned was invaluable. Another great aspect of having a good accountant is that they may have other clients you could network with. They may know of someone in the same business to partner with or who would provide services that you are looking for.

In the end, having a conversation with my accountant gave me more resolve that I was doing the right thing by quitting my job. Depending on your business, it may be good to talk with an accountant to see what you may need to prepare for before you quit.

TAKE ACTION

What are your weaknesses that you should have someone else do rather than you spending your time and energy on?

1. ______________________________
2. ______________________________
3. ______________________________
4. ______________________________
5. ______________________________

Who can help you fill in these weak spots?

1. ______________________________
2. ______________________________
3. ______________________________

Think of the B.R.R.R.R. strategy I use for my business. What creative ways can you think of that will help you to build your business faster? Write them down below and how you will implement these ideas:

____

____

____

____

____

____

____

CHAPTER NINETEEN

LESSON 16

PLAN FOR FUTURE EMERGENCIES

"Before dreaming about the future or marking plans, you need to articulate what you already have going for you – as entrepreneurs do."

– Reid Hoffman

The business was doing the opposite of what it was supposed to do.

Instead of making me money, the business was costing me money. Month after month, the paycheck I earned from my job was being poured into the business as I was trying to keep it afloat. No matter what I did or how much money I put into the business, it continued to eat up cash.

Life is like a dream when a business is making money, but it can be a nightmare when it is not. The day I sold my business, I was relieved. The expenses, time burden, opportunity cost, and the responsibility of employing people were a lot to manage. Add onto that, the business was taking money out of my pocket every month.

If I had not planned for potential future problems for Downtown Express, I may not have been able to hold onto the business long enough to sell it. Even though I believed my business was going to make me money, I was prepared for it not to. Praise the Lord we had enough money saved for emergencies such as this. If we didn't have the next month's rent, the new buyer may not have followed through with the purchase, or the landlord may not have extended the lease to the new buyer. Many things could have gone wrong if we didn't plan for hard times.

Emergencies happen. It is a fact of life.

How you prepare for those emergencies will prove how successful you are at being an entrepreneur. Planning for your future income, expenses, and emergencies just might be what saves you from closing down your business in the end. The best time to plan for hard times is when things are going well. It is already too late to plan once things are going bad for you and your business. Learn from my mistakes and plan ahead.

If you fail to plan, you plan to fail.

Have Enough Income Coming In from Your Business

In my "How to Quit Your Job" series of books, I explain that replacing your job income with your business income is the key to quitting your job. We all have expenses and those expenses need to be paid, whether we like them or not. Without adequate income coming in from your business to pay your bills, you will become bankrupt and eventually need to get a job again.

Now is the time to take a hard look at your income and expenses. If you need to, ask an accountant to help you put together all the information. This will show you if you have enough income coming in from your business to fulfill your obligations and expenses. As an entrepreneur, some months, the income will be better than others. Most of the time, your income will fluctuate on a month to month basis. You must account for the monthly up's and down's.

Here is how you can plan for your future income. Take an average of the most recent 6 to 8 month's income and expenses for your business. Include your personal expenses as well to get an accurate number for your life. Add up all the income for each month. Do the same for your expenses.

Income example:		Expense example:	
Month 1 Income:	$ 6,500	Month 1 Expense:	$ 4,000
Month 2 Income:	$ 6,800	Month 2 Expense:	$ 3,800
Month 3 Income:	$ 4,600	Month 3 Expense:	$ 4,500
Month 4 Income:	$ 6,900	Month 4 Expense:	$ 5,300
Month 5 Income:	$ 2,200	Month 5 Expense:	$ 6,200
Month 6 Income:	$ 4,500	Month 6 Expense:	$ 5,500
Total Income:	**$31,500**	**Total Expense:**	**$29,300**

In this example, the total income exceeds the total expenses by $2,200. This $2,200 is your total profit after 6 months.

Looking at this example month by month, you may notice that some months have a profit and some months have a loss. In the first two months here, profit is $5,500 over the expenses. At first glance, this is great news. Your business is making good money after two months. The mistake would be to think that this is extra money that you can spend and not save for the future.

Remember my story of how I overspent and under earned? My rental property business was doing very well, until it didn't. Those three months with negative income were drastically detrimental to my overall goal of quitting my job. The money was rolling in so I didn't prepare for the months with little to no income. My mistake was that I thought I could spend all the excess. I was wrong.

You may think to yourself, "My business is doing great! These profits should continue and I deserve to spend that profit. I'm taking my family on a Disney Cruise!" This type of thinking could be very harmful to your goals.

I'm not saying that you shouldn't go on the Disney Cruise with your family. I am also not saying that you shouldn't spend your profits as you see fit. Actually, being successfully unemployed will allow you to do just that. Spend money to do the things you want to do AND have the time to do it. But, in order to do so, you must plan for the ups-and-downs of your business income. Now, back to the scenario of the two profitable months.

Let's say that you decide to take this $5,500 and spend it on a cruise for your family. You spend the entire $5,500. Then on the cruise, you decide to buy your spouse a present for $1,500. After the super fun trip is all over, you have great memories, a present for your spouse and are now $1,500 in the negative for your income.

Now, look at month 5 with the negative income of $4,000. This may have been a very off month and your business took a big hit. If you plan ahead for these bad months, the good months will help to balance out loss in profits. If you had spent that $5,500 on the cruise and the extra $1,500 on the present, you would now be in debt. Looking ahead to the six-month total income and expenses, instead of being $2,200 positive in cash after six months, you would now be $4,800 in debt.

The point is that being a business owner and entrepreneur, you need to change the way you think about your income. Gone are the days of a steady paycheck just because you gave your employer 40 hours of your life each week. Your income will now fluctuate with your business. Some months will be good and some will be bad. If you plan ahead and build your business well, you will have enough money to live on and plan for the future.

Find the Average Monthly Amount

When planning for the future, it would be best to have an average monthly budget with a fixed amount that you can spend. With that number in mind, you should safely be able to spend this amount each month.

With the example above, now take the total income and expenses and divide them by 6 months to get the average each month.

Total Income: $31,500 / 6 months = $5,250 average monthly income
Total Expense: $29,300 / 6 months = $4,883 average monthly expense

The average profit is the average income minus the average expense.

Average Monthly Income - Average Monthly Expense = Average Profit
$5,250 - $4,883 = $367 Average Monthly Profit

So, your average monthly profit that you can spend, invest, or save, would be $367 a month. Now, instead of spending the $5,500 on the Disney Cruise, a good idea may be to start saving the $367 a month to pay for the Disney Cruise at a future date when you have all the money saved for the trip.

Create A Budget (and stick to it!)

If you don't plan where your money should go each month, you will wonder where it went.

Having a budget that charts your income and expenses is a very wise thing to do. It will help you plan for those ups and downs with your business income. As you are now planning to quit your job, one of the very first things you must do is create a budget.

Download the quick budget worksheet and fill it out if you haven't already. Get it here: http://www.masterpassiveincome.com/quickbudget

It is quick and easy and will allow you to see if your income exceeds your expenses.

The goal of a budget is to ensure that your income is greater than your expenses. In the last section, we saw how living on your business income is not like a paycheck. Some months are better than others and some months are worse than others. Just like how I received a fraction of money from my rental property business, you too could expect $6000 a month from your business income but only bring in $17. For me, by having a budget, sticking to it, and the by the grace of God, we were able to weather the storm of those hard months. Even though it set me back an entire year from my goal.

Once you have the quick budget worksheet done, you can stop there or move onto a more sophisticated budgeting software. For those of you who want or need something more robust, the next step for you is to get a budgeting program like YNAB.com or You Need A Budget. This program is terrific and will help you to create an amazing budget that will plan for life without a steady paycheck.

THE GOAL OF YOUR BUDGET IS TO ENSURE THAT YOUR INCOME IS GREATER THAN YOUR EXPENSES.

Here are the four rules you need for your budget:

1. Give Every Dollar a Job
2. Save for a Rainy Day
3. Roll with the Punches
4. Live on Last Month's Income

With these rules, you will learn to live on a budget to keep your expenses in check. Also, learn from my mistake and don't fall into the trap of thinking the good days will always keep coming. There will be times where your income does not come in like you thought. Be prepared with a budget that will help you weather those storms.

Emergency Fund

As explained before, because your one income does not depend on the hours you work, your income will vary from month to month. Some months may be so rough that you will need extra money to pay your bills. This is where an emergency fund comes into place. An emergency fund is an account with designated money set aside for emergencies. It can be cash under your mattress or a separate bank account. Either way, having money set aside for a rainy day will help you to get past these.

Without an emergency fund, I would not have had enough money to hold onto my business, Downtown Express, long enough to sell it.

This emergency fund should only be used in case of an emergency. Think of it as an emergency parachute. It is better to have one and not need it than need it and not have one.

So, how do you set up an emergency fund?

There are many different thoughts about how to plan for an emergency fund. You can go by your expenses, your income, your future purchases, etc. The best way I have seen to plan for an emergency fund is to have three to six months of expenses saved. This would be any and all expenses you and your business will have during an average month. If you went through your income and expenses when you created a budget, you are almost done with this part.

If your total expenses for you and your business is $4500 a month, you will use that amount and multiply it by how many months you think you may be without any income if there is an emergency. If you want to be on the safe side, I recommend having six months saved. You could have less, but you are probably not as prepared as you should be.

For the $4,500 per month example, a six-month emergency fund should have $27,000.

I know, I know. You may say to me, "$27,000 is a lot of money to save up! How will I ever get that much?" Honestly, if you are asking that question, I suggest you put more effort into building your business to make more money. When you make more money, you tackle two potential problems.

1. You are able to save more money faster to fund your emergency account.
2. You now have a stronger business which leads to increased income.

A quick suggestion on where you should hold your emergency fund for good interest AND still have access to it. I suggest keeping your money where I personally keep my money. Capital One 360. They give generous interest rates for checking and savings. Currently, they give 0.1% for a money market account each month. http://www.masterpassiveincome.com/capitalink

With the example of $27,000 saved in an emergency fund, you will probably earn about $10 a month in interest. It is not all that much, but it is $10 more than you had last month. A normal savings account at Chase, Bank of America, or Wells Fargo, it will take you the entire year to earn $10 in interest.

By having an emergency fund and a budget, you will plan well for future problems that may occur.

TAKE ACTION

Take an average of 6-8 months of your previous income to find your average monthly income:

$ ________________________________

Take and average of 6-8 months of your previous expenses to find your average monthly expenses:

$ ________________________________

Find out how much should you save in the bank as an emergency fund.

The minimum advised emergency fund should be three months of your monthly expenses saved.

Total Monthly Expenses: $____________________

Multiply Expenses by 3 months: $____________________

The maximum advised emergency fund should be six months of your monthly expenses saved.

Total Monthly Expenses: $____________________

Multiply Expenses by 6 months: $____________________

Make a commitment to yourself to save up 3-6 months of your expenses in an interest baring bank account at Capital One as an emergency fund. http://www.masterpassiveincome.com/capitalink

____

Signature Date

CHAPTER TWENTY

FINISH SUCCESSFULLY

"Every accomplishment starts with a decision to try."
– Unknown

As I have already said, you are worth much more than any job can pay you.

Now it is up to you to prove it. Not to me, but to yourself. I already know that you are more valuable than your job because I proved it to myself. Just three months after I quit my job, I made three times as much money from my businesses than I ever did from my job. And this is just the start. If I did that in just three months, imagine how much money I will be making in three years.

This is your future as an entrepreneur. As you plan and build your businesses to be successful, you will be able to quit your job and make so much more money than you ever could working for someone else. It is my hope that you now have a new understanding of the possibility that YOU TOO can quit your job.

If you haven't already started your business, it is up to you to find, develop, build, and grow your business big enough to replace the income from your job. No matter what business you choose, you are now an entrepreneur in the making. If you already have your business, think like an entrepreneur and solve the problems that are standing in the way of quitting your job.

Now that you have finished the 16 lessons, it is time for you to apply them to your business and life. If you are going to successfully quit your job, you need to put these plans into practice and actively work for your success. The application of these lessons will take time but it will be all worth it in the end. Focus on being intentional in implementing them into your business.

The only thing left for you now is to get to work and plan how you can be successfully unemployed.

WANTREPRENEURS DREAM ABOUT QUITTING THEIR JOB. ENTREPRENEURS ACTUALLY DO IT.

Make the commitment to yourself today that you will quit your job and let nothing hinder you from living the life of your dreams.

Don't Forget Your Free Bonus!

Just to say thank you for buying this book, I'd like to give you TWO free bonuses absolutely **FREE**.

- Bonus 17th Lesson: Managing Your Business Finances

- The Successfully Unemployed Workbook

GET YOUR AMAZING BONUSES FOR "Successfully Unemployed" 100% FREE!

DOWNLOAD FREE INSTANTLY HERE

http://www.masterpassiveincome.com/SUbonus

About the Author

Since making the decision to be independent and quit his job, Dustin took just 9 years to accomplish his goal because of his passive income businesses. As a businessman and entrepreneur, he has learned what it takes to build a thriving business that brings in monthly cash flow every month. As a life-long learner with a desire to build bigger and better businesses, he continues to grow his wealth and independence from ever working for someone again.

In 2006, Dustin married Melissa, the love of his life, and continue to live in Phoenix Arizona. They both work together on their passive income businesses and they continue to be successfully married with their four children.

Dustin has a passion and a gift of teaching the things he is passionate about. He enjoys helping others achieve success in all areas of life and encourages them to push through their limiting beliefs that are holding them back. Countless others have learned how to use passive income to bring in monthly cash flow with his help.

He has already quit his job and lives the dream every day. He is the founder of Master Passive Income, a company dedicated to helping people achieve financial freedom with passive income.

Dustin and his lovely wife Melissa have four children and are blessed by the Lord to be saved by His grace.

Get 50% OFF the Other Books Written
By Dustin Heiner

How to Quit Your Job with Passive Income

The Ultimate Beginners Guide to Wealth and Riches with 12 Proven Businesses You Can Start Today

In today's world, we all are expected to live our lives working for someone else. Working 40+ hours a week at a job you hate, for a boss that is horrible, and wasting your life away for a paycheck. But there is a book that will help you escape the rat race of life and ditch the cubicle, assembly line, or dead-end job.

How to Quit Your Job with Passive Income has been proven to help many people learn the secrets of passive income that only those who are already rich know. This book has been designed to help guide you through the process of being an employee earning a wage, to a business owner with multiple streams of passive income.

How to Quit Your Job with Rental Properties

A Step-by-Step guide to Passive Income by Investing in Real Estate

The problem that affects almost everyone today is being stuck in a career they hate. People are conditioned to work their lives away for someone else and only get paid for the hour they work. How would you like to quit your job today because you have enough passive income to live on?

This book contains step-by-step training to help you acquire rental properties to allow you to quit your job and be financially free so you will never have to work again. Designed for the newbie or seasoned pro, anyone will learn how they can earn passive income from rental properties and quit their job.

Lasting Marriage

Discovering God's Meaning and Purpose for Your Relationship

Is your marriage living the true meaning and purpose of marriage? Do you want your marriage to last through all that life throws at you?

Would you like to see your marriage benefit from having more love, joy, and intimacy?

Lasting Marriage is an encouraging and insightful book that will help your marriage grow and strengthen in love and service to each other. You will learn how your marriage can become one of those success stories you hear about. You will be more in love with your spouse at your 50th wedding anniversary than on your wedding day. By knowing and applying God's meaning and purpose of marriage into your relationship, you will have a lasting marriage.

Get the PDF version of these other books

50% off the retail price.

GO TO: www.masterpassiveincome.com/pdf-books

and use the promo code "halfoff" to receive a 50% discount on the retail price for finishing this book.

Will You Help Others Learn These Lessons Too?

If you enjoyed Successfully Unemployed, would you mind taking a minute to write a quick review? Even a short review helps, and it'd mean a lot to me. The more positive reviews this book has, the more these retailers will help others see it and hopefully read it.

Please go here to give an honest review:
http://www.masterpassiveincome.com/SUReview

Finally, if you'd like to get free bonus materials from this book and receive updates on my future projects, you can sign up for the Master Passive Income newsletter at www.MasterPassiveIncome.com

You can also follow me and Master Passive Income on Twitter and Facebook.

Facebook: http://www.facebook.com/masterpassiveinc/
Twitter: http://www.twitter.com/mpidustinheiner

I WANT YOU TO QUIT YOUR JOB TOO!

Made in the USA
San Bernardino, CA
30 December 2017